Overcoming

OBESITY

in Childhood and Adolescence

To my wife, Sandy—my inspiration, my love;
to my father—I stand on your shoulders;
and in memory of my mother, my teacher
Don
To Patsy and Alex—my continual source of love and energy
Allen

Overcoming OBESITY
in Childhood and Adolescence

A Guide for
School Leaders

A JOINT PUBLICATION

NATIONAL ASSOCIATION OF ELEMENTARY SCHOOL PRINCIPALS
Serving All Elementary and Middle Level Principals

CORWIN PRESS

Donald
SCHUMACHER

J. Allen
QUEEN

CORWIN PRESS
A SAGE Publications Company
Thousand Oaks, CA 91320

For information:

Corwin Press
A Sage Publications Company
2455 Teller Road
Thousand Oaks, California 91320
www.corwinpress.com

Sage Publications Ltd.
1 Oliver's Yard
55 City Road
London EC1Y 1SP
United Kingdom

Sage Publications India Pvt. Ltd.
B-42, Panchsheel Enclave
Post Box 4109
New Delhi 110 017 India

Printed in the United States of America

Library of Congress Cataloging-in-Publication Data

Schumacher, Donald.
Overcoming obesity in childhood and adolescence : a guide for school leaders / Donald Schumacher and J. Allen Queen.
    p. cm.
Includes bibliographical references and index.
ISBN 1-4129-1665-8 or 978-1-4129-1665-3 (cloth : alk. paper)
ISBN 1-4129-1666-6 or 978-1-4129-1666-0 (pbk. : alk. paper)
    1. Obesity in children—United States. 2. Children—Nutrition—United States. 3. Health promotion—United States. 4. School management and organization—United States. I. Queen, J. Allen. II. Title.
RJ399.C6S38 2007
618.92'398—dc22   2006016034

This book is printed on acid-free paper.

06   07   08   09   10   10   9   8   7   6   5   4   3   2   1

Acquisitions Editor:	Faye Zucker
Editorial Assistant:	Gem Rabanera
Production Editor:	Libby Larson
Copy Editor:	Brenda Weight
Typesetter:	C&M Digitals (P) Ltd.
Proofreader:	Mary Meagher
Indexer:	Rick Hurd
Cover Designer:	Scott Van Atta

Contents

Preface   vii

Acknowledgments   xi

About the Authors   xiii

1. **Childhood Obesity, Schools, and Society**   **1**
   The Essential Truths   1
   Practical Guides to the Essential Truths   2

2. **The Principal's Role as an Agent of Change**   **23**
   The Essential Truths   24
   Practical Guides to the Essential Truths   25

3. **The Barriers We Face**   **55**
   The Essential Truths   55
   Practical Guides to the Essential Truths   56
   Schools Are Negative Exercise Zones   68
   School Board, Board of Education,
       and Parent Organizations as Barriers   68
   Health Care Provider Knowledge
       Base and Involvement as a Barrier   69

4. **School Principal Action Plans**   **71**
   The Essential Truths   71
   Practical Guides to the Essential Truths   71

5. **Maximizing Principal, Teacher, and
   Student Plans for Nutritional
   Improvement and Physical Fitness**   **107**
   Making the Grade   108

Beyond Instructional Leadership 109
A Personal Word About Your Health and Stress 110

**Resource A. Nutritional and Physical
Fitness Survey for Grades 3–5** **115**

**Resource B. Nutritional and Physical
Fitness Survey for Grades 6–12** **121**

**Resource C. Approximate
Calories Burned Per Hour** **127**

Resource D. USDA Label Definitions **129**

References **131**

Index **135**

Preface

Over 60% of the adult population in America is overweight or obese. As shocking as this fact is, the real problem is the lack of a plan that works for everyone. There will never be such a plan. The problem is too complex for a generic answer and, as a result, adults are having trouble dealing with significant lifestyle decisions that need to be made to improve unhealthy weight. There is no quick fix and American adults have a problem with that. Even more alarming is the unhealthy weight of our children and adolescents. Overweight in our youth is galloping along out of control, in epidemic proportions. In 2004, Brownell and Horgen warned us that "American children may be the first generation in modern history to live shorter lives than their parents." The authors estimate that 16% to 40% of elementary school children are joining the ranks of being overweight or seriously overweight.

Body Mass Index (BMI) is the height-to-weight ratio measurement physicians use in adults and school-age children to define weight status. In our youth, however, BMI is expressed as a percentile based on sex and age. A BMI in the 85th percentile or higher defines students at risk for an unhealthy weight. The higher the BMI percentile over the 85th, the greater the risk of developing serious medical problems that are weight related. The numbers are staggering when you consider that there are 9 million youngsters at a serious weight health risk.

Calling the problem of obesity an ignored public health problem, a spokesperson for the World Health Organization (WHO) warned that millions would experience a variety of serious health disorders (World Health Organization [WHO], 2003). Julie Gerberding, director of the Centers for Disease Control and Prevention (CDC) asserted that the obesity epidemic is more harmful than any other epidemic in our history ("Americans Experiencing Pandemic," 2003). Now with the problem dubbed "the childhood obesity epidemic," we are beginning to address the factors promoting unhealthy weight and much attention is falling upon the role to be played by elementary, middle school, and senior high school principals.

The Child Nutrition Act is a $16 billion federal bill under the National School Lunch Program, signed into law by President Bush in June of 2004. The new law expands upon policies for better nutrition in the federally funded school breakfast and lunch programs. This act requires that all school districts must develop and adopt written "wellness policies" by July 1, 2006. These policies are to be designed and implemented for the 2006–2007 school year with established written goals for nutrition. Included within the plan are quality statements for guiding educators in the instructional aspects of nutritional education and guidelines for all foods.

The Child Nutrition Act of 2004 also requires the schools to establish programs and procedures to follow for increasing physical activity in the classrooms. Many districts do not have this policy in place, and principals should be aware that their state's Department of Public Instruction or Local Educational Agency may have additional requirements. Similar to many things educators must do in the schools, the authors know that schools will be looked upon to be a major help in this childhood epidemic. And they should! No other public institution has the ability to pull off such a high stakes and, perhaps, life-extending goal. School principals are already burdened by leadership roles in issues such as increased student poverty, negative imaging by the media, growing teacher shortages, and standards and expectations to meet state mandates and district expectations of the No Child Left Behind Act. They must now take the lead in waging a war on childhood obesity and lead their teachers and students into that arena. In this book, the authors have provided much of the background and insight and many of the tools needed to make an impact on the goal of healthy weight for all children in every school in America.

In Chapter 1, we discuss the importance of childhood obesity in our society by exploring what we call in each chapter, "The Essential Truths." We sift through the confusing, often inaccurate, sometimes bogus misinformation available to the public and focus on the science behind the number one public health problem of the twenty-first century. We address unhealthy weight in our youth as a continuum from overweight to obesity and we discuss the extent of unhealthy student population in your schools. We review how the negative impact of childhood obesity touches every aspect of a student's life. There are social and psychological issues, peer group discrimination, and prejudice that interfere with the academic potential. A case study is presented.

The Essential Truths of Chapter 2 are dedicated to the principal's role as an agent of change in the prevention and education in this epidemic of overweight and obese students. A principal's responsibility for guiding and developing the school's vision for overall student success is discussed. The chapter emphasizes the importance of your leadership in the implementation of the related and newly required state, federal, and district laws and standards, all within the framework of the academic school day.

The Essential Truths in this chapter emphasize that the principal must be a positive role model for staff and students alike. You will learn who are facilitators and who could be saboteurs. A healthy role model requires having the tools needed to make changes. What tools are needed and how do you make the necessary changes? How do you identify those staff members who may have trouble changing? You will be given a step-by-step tutorial in the behavioral, nutritional, and exercise aspects needed to attain or to maintain a healthy weight and lifestyle. A wellness and staff development plan for teachers and staff is described, including training opportunities to learn concepts in health and wellness and instructional techniques for implementing integrated instruction within the classroom. Changes in the school environment to support healthy weight habits in the classroom and with teachers are also outlined.

In Chapter 3, the barriers that principals must recognize are outlined. The Essential Truths here include becoming a positive role model and dealing with parental resistance and student prejudice and lack of student understanding of why they should care about their own personal health. The structural barriers of the school environment are significant. We discuss what can be done. Stress and roadblocks to readiness to change are highlighted.

In Chapter 4, the focus is on action plans for the school principal. The Essential Truths of this chapter center on developmental aspects of a faculty health promotion plan, plus a plan to improve the health of students, including those aspects that impact childhood psychosocial and emotional development. Who should be involved in plan development? How do you organize such plans? Our answers are in this chapter. Details about how to integrate health and wellness into classroom instruction are presented. How changes in the law will affect you are put into the perspective of what you will be able to accomplish with the insight you will gain from this chapter. Rule changes and new school administrative and classroom teacher responsibilities and obligations have the potential to overburden you and your staff if you are unaware of how to organize a plan of action.

Chapter 5 concentrates on a guide for understanding stress of principals and includes direct, palliative, cognitive, and physical strategies for coping with stress. A stress wellness plan outlined for teachers and staff is organized to be implemented in the school.

Acknowledgments

A special thanks to Faye Zucker, our wonderful editor, who was instrumental in causing this book to be considered as the alpha book for the new Book of the Month Club for the members of the National Association of Elementary School Principals. We also acknowledge the contributions of the leadership and staff of Corwin Press and the National Association of Elementary School Principals for their joint venture in publishing this book as a useful tool for school leaders. We also wish to thank Brenda and Libby for their editorial assistance. Special thanks to Alex Queen for his numerous hours of editing and proofreading.

Corwin Press thanks the following individuals for their contributions to this book:

Gloria DePaul, NBPTS:ECYA/School Counseling, Tampa, FL

James Gostomski, M.ED, NBCT, Physical Education Teacher, Verde Elementary, Boca Raton, FL

Dolores Huffman, Associate Professor of Nursing, Purdue University Calumet, Highland, IN

Stephanie A. Slowik, M.ED., NBCT, School Counselor, West Lake Elementary School, Cary, NC

About the Authors

**Donald Schumacher, MD,** is the cofounder and Medical Director of the Center for Nutrition & Preventive Medicine in Charlotte, North Carolina. His medical training has been at the University of Bologna in Italy, University of Pennsylvania Graduate Hospital in Philadelphia for internship, and internal medicine residency at Georgetown University Hospital in Washington, DC. He is a past president of the American Heart Association in Mecklenburg County, North Carolina. His major research interests are in obesity management in adults and childhood and in cholesterol abnormalities. He is nationally known and is a sought-after speaker to medical groups. His publications have appeared in national medical peer review journals. He developed a 16-part obesity series that aired for public television in Charlotte, North Carolina, and in other areas of the country coast to coast. His work was featured in an *ABC 20/20* story, as well as in interviews in other national television programs. Dr. Schumacher serves on a state of state committee for childhood obesity. He has presented information and research data on obesity in front of an FDA panel. He has a passion for educating the general public on medical topics and has done so regularly on radio and television. He is the author of the *WIN (What I Need—to Succeed)* manual, the basis for weight management strategies used at the Center for Nutrition & Preventive Medicine.

 **J. Allen Queen, EdD,** is Professor and past Chair of the Department of Educational Leadership at the University of North Carolina at Charlotte. His publications include *The Block Scheduling Handbook* (2003), *The 4x4 Block Schedule* (1998), *Complete Karate* (1994), four other fitness titles for young readers, many journal articles, and hundreds of presentations to educational groups interested in instructional leadership, effective time management, and wellness.

Dr. Queen is an educational consultant to over 250 school districts in 44 states in the United States and numerous schools and universities in 5 foreign countries. He lives with his wife, Patsy, in Kings Mountain, North Carolina, and can be reached by e-mail at Stopchildhoodobesity@yahoo.com.

CHAPTER ONE

Childhood Obesity, Schools, and Society

Critical Question 1

Just how important is this issue of childhood obesity in our society?

THE ESSENTIAL TRUTHS

1.1. Childhood obesity is the number one public health problem of the twenty-first century.

1.2. In some children, there is a direct continuum from being overweight to becoming obese, and overweight children are at higher risk for becoming obese adults.

1.3. In your school, at least one out of four students is at an unhealthy weight.

1.4. Unhealthy weight of students has a major negative impact on their personal health and wellness.

1.5. Unhealthy weight impacts the academic achievement and emotional-social development of students.

PRACTICAL GUIDES TO
THE ESSENTIAL TRUTHS

1.1. Childhood obesity is the number one public health problem of the twenty-first century.

Some school children have medical problems that can be recognized by direct observation, such as eyeglasses, a body deformity, a bandaged ankle, facial characteristics of Down's syndrome, a cast on an arm—or excess weight. All provoke some degree of sympathy, but while you might ask a child with a cast, "What happened to you?" when you see the overweight child, you may think, "Why did you let that happen to your body? Where were your parents?" The reality is that being at an unhealthy weight is not simply a matter of self-neglect or self-control. It is much more complicated.

If there were obvious answers to why an increasing number of our children are becoming overweight, we would not be in the middle of an unhealthy weight epidemic. If there were obvious answers, parents and other caregivers would be able to intervene in the weight proliferation of our youth. If there were obvious answers, more than 61% of American adults would not have an overweight problem. If there were obvious answers, we would have corrected the overweight status of 2- to 5-year-olds—with 10% from this group being at an unhealthy weight and 16% of adolescents in the same predicament. These percentages will continue to increase as our nation gets fatter.

Locating, examining, and assessing the vast amount of instructional material in print and on the Web for practical use for school principals and teachers is an overwhelming job. Trying to then tease out the inaccurate materials may take someone with large amounts of time and medical and nutritional degrees. We have sifted through the many volumes to get to the essence of truth. With what we collected, selected, and designed, multiplied by our many years of experience in medical and educational practice and research as a physician and a principal, we have made the process more readily available to you and have identified what we believe will become known as "best practice" in this emerging field.

Lack of information about obesity is certainly not the problem, but with an overload of confusing and often conflicting information about nutrition, exercise, and lifestyle, however, reliable resources must be identified. Information is available both from credible and questionable sources. Bogus sources may be hard to identify, making it difficult to know what to trust, to follow, or to teach. With the correct materials, you must ultimately and directly address the weight problems of your students, and, perhaps, indirectly or directly address the weight problems of their teachers.

Exercise, for example, is a vital part of weight control, but information that claims rapid changes in muscle bulk and improvement in specific muscle groups by using a certain piece of exercise equipment should be considered suspect. Testimonials have no validity as proof of effectiveness in managing any aspect of being overweight or obese. Because we are all different, there is no best eating and exercise plan to lose weight. If the perfect approach existed, the national obesity crisis affecting more than 61% of adults and nearly 40% of children would either not exist or would come to an abrupt ending. School children are just as diverse as adults but are even less in control of their lives. The approach to the weight problem addressed during school must be based on science and broad enough in approach to protect students from becoming overweight and to help those in need of losing weight. With this focus, the overweight child is not isolated and the normal-weight child is reinforced.

Childhood and adolescent overweight and obesity are public health concerns of such magnitude that unhealthy weight is rapidly becoming the most prevalent nutrition problem of this age group in America and worldwide, according to William Dietz, MD, of the Centers for Disease Control (CDC). In fact, food-related diseases are the second leading cause of preventable death in the United States, and are readily poised to overtake the leading cause, cigarette smoking. William Dietz testified before the Committee on Health, Education, Labor, and Pensions Sub-committee on Public Health, U.S. Senate, that 60% of overweight children have at least one additional cardiovascular disease risk factor, and 25% have two or more heart-related risk factors (Dietz, Bland, Gortmaker, Molloy & Schmid, 2002). In a few words, the more weight gained, the more danger of developing medical complications. The causes of the childhood obesity epidemic and of weight problems among the entire population are beginning to be unraveled. Since the medical and environmental components are intertwined, the problem is both multiplex and difficult to treat.

Why is this happening to our children? The answer is complex and not yet fully understood. However, we do know there is a dynamic interaction between our brain and other body control mechanisms located in our muscles, stomach and intestinal tract, and organs such as the pancreas, liver, and even the fat cells. Hormones, enzymes, other body chemicals, and neurotransmitters play roles in trying to keep body fat content at a constant amount. Sometimes this control mechanism gets out of balance, and the body accumulates extra fat. There are both internal and external forces at play when this occurs. One force is our inherited makeup, that is, our body's potential to turn on our own latent obesity genes. Other components include family dynamics and social and environmental factors. Some of these factors are a constant, while others can, and usually do, change over time. As individual human beings, we are no better than our own unique family tree when it comes to inherited risks. Although the numbers vary from study to study, it is clear that when both parents are obese, almost 70% of their children have a high potential to become obese adolescents. If one parent is obese, 50% of their children have the same potential. This disease is so pervasive in our society that even if neither parent is obese, 9% of their children will potentially become obese adolescents. Children who are overweight have a higher probability of having overweight siblings. This family trait phenomenon is quite obvious to almost any observer. Anybody attending a family reunion of a non–family member has seen this phenomenon directly. Similarities in body shape as well as voice inflection, skin tone, and mannerisms are but a few characteristics that a family may share.

"Childhood and adolescent overweight and obesity are public health concerns of such magnitude that unhealthy weight is rapidly becoming the most prevalent nutrition problem of this age group in America and worldwide."

For most of us, it is when genetics and an unhealthy lifestyle merge that weight gain begins. When the balance between incoming energy (what we eat) and outgoing energy (how active we are) gets out of phase, weight gain begins.

There are, however, the fortunate few who are genetically resistant to weight gain. Some of these people have the hardest time understanding obesity and may be the most critical toward overweight individuals. Skinny people are not better people, but they are luckier than those with a weight problem. Life functions such as pulse, blood pressure, breathing, sleeping patterns, bowel frequency, body weight, and even hunger are maintained as regularly as possible by the brain. Intricate and multileveled internal control mechanisms work as checks and balances to make the body harmony happen. This is known as homeostasis.

When our eating choices become less healthy and portions increase, we can lose some of our steady state mode. If at the same time we are not leading an active lifestyle, including structured physical activity, we will stop burning off excess fat and go into a fat storage, weight gain mode. The weight gain can be slow and progressive or seem to occur rapidly. With our body's tremendous capacity to store body fat, the problem can become a lifelong journey of gaining weight. Unfortunately, the overconsumption of calories and underutilization of calorie burning lead to excess energy being stored as body fat much more than muscle mass. Weight gain is usually a combination of fat and muscle, with fat predominating. Any lifestyle change that affects eating or activity patterns can potentially turn on a weight gain phase. As a result, we are witnessing and participating in the fattening of America, and we are putting our youngest generation at the greatest risk in history. A fact: we truly are both what we eat and how energetically we use our time, and we are quickly learning that poor eating habits and limited physical activity can play a direct role in the path to obesity.

1.2. In some children, there is a direct continuum from being overweight to becoming obese, and overweight children are at higher risk for becoming obese adults.

The difference between an overweight and an obese student is a matter of degree. In reality, obesity is a progression from normal to overweight, and, if initiated after the age of 6, and certainly during adolescence, it can lead to obesity in young adulthood that extends throughout life. The significant health and social consequences are a concern for both the developed and third world countries in what the World Health Organization calls a "global epidemic." As poorer countries are introduced to modern Western ways, both weight gain and overweight are direct by-products from this change.

What will be required to break the cycle of obesity includes discipline, focus, and a willingness to change. It will require a redefinition and acceptance of what is healthy weight. The body shapes found in magazines and portrayed as normal in music, television, and movie celebrities present greatly distorted messages for children and adolescents. Most of us, as medical and education personnel, know that these body images are unrealistic, unhealthy, and misrepresentative of a reasonable weight. Instead, these represent a formula for failure, further encouraging unrealistic goals. Our youth, however, are greatly influenced by these images and the implied messages of related success. All educators strive for their students to succeed. We can play a role in educating about weight distortion, body image, healthy eating, and exercise, especially if such education will give the gift of a more self-confident student. The changes needed for our youth to be healthy must occur at the personal, communal, and societal levels. If changes are not made, then the next generation of children may not be able to afford the cost of their own health care due to the many medical complications of obesity. In fact, we strongly believe that without a major change in direction, the current generation of parents will most likely outlive their children—a frightening thought! If current projections continue and the epidemic is not stopped, related diabetes and heart disease will shorten children's lives by 20 to 40 years.

Overweight and obesity can be a continuum; weight usually increases over time, punctuated by intermittent periods of weight stability, weight gain, and even transient weight loss. The more unhealthy weight gained, the greater danger of developing medical complications. During childhood, however, weight loss is not always the goal. For younger children, prevention of unhealthy weight gain may be enough. For an overweight child, becoming thinner may mean growing into his or her correct weight, which occurs as the child grows in height along with increasing the muscle mass for support. Keeping weight stable, or having a proportional weight gain and spreading it over a longer body frame, occurs with children who are still in their height and growth phase. Before the ages of 4 to 6, a higher weight may not be a potential marker of a lifelong overweight problem. By preventing or correcting abnormal overweight in school-age children, we can slow down the obesity problem that is spreading through our youngest generation. Understand that this is a problem that is out of control, and if not harnessed, it will undermine the health improvements modern medicine has made to date.

1.3. In your school, at least one out of four students is at an unhealthy weight.

Unhealthy weight in our schoolchildren is moving beyond 27%. That is an incredibly large number from a medical standpoint, and there is every indication that it will increase unless we do something about it. The rise has been steady and alarming since the late 1960s and more aggressive in the last two decades. It has been estimated that with the trend toward larger portions of food, less exercise, and inattention to the growing problem, about the same number of children and adolescents who are not currently overweight are at risk for becoming overweight (Ogden, Flegal, Carroll, & Johnson, 2002).

Of these overweight elementary, middle, and high school students, as much as 70% to 80% have the potential to become overweight or obese adults. There are CDC– and American Pediatric Society–approved pediatric charts available to compare age and sex with height and weight to determine weight definitions for underweight, normal weight, overweight, and severely over-

> "Unfortunately, the limited daily activity of children at school would not meet the lowest of standards. In fact, in most schools, physical activity is barely more than walking in and out of the school."

weight. The word *obesity* is not currently used publicly when discussing school-age children. It is considered too derogatory and offensive. These charts use BMI (body mass index) as the representative value for defining these weight categories. BMI is a mathematical representation of relative body fat content. For most individuals, the more the body fat, the higher the BMI, whether child or adult. There are exceptions to this BMI rule for those individuals who are very short, very tall, or very muscular. The Asian population is considered overweight or obese at lower BMI numbers than other ethnic groups.

Being overweight (having an elevated BMI) is a marker for potential or already-existing health problems that are associated with carrying too much body fat. Body shape is a visual reminder of the social, physical, and psychological problems that may coexist. Being an overweight student may affect academic and behavioral performance at school. Having an overweight child in school should alert a principal to potential discrimination from classmates and even from classroom teachers.

The prevalence of obesity is increasing at an alarming rate with no end in sight. In children and adolescents, it has doubled in the last two decades, and 13% of 6- to 11-year-olds and 15.5% of 12- to 19-year-olds have BMI levels in the severely overweight category. In the school-age population, changes must be directed toward maintaining a healthy weight and maintaining muscle without sacrificing body growth and development. Regular eating times are mandatory, with minimal sweet snacks, drinks, and desserts. Exercise is important, but unfortunately, the limited daily activity of children at school would not meet the lowest of standards. In fact, in most schools, physical activity is barely more than walking in and out of the school. Due to limitations of space in this book, we recommend that readers view Web sites that list ages, heights, and weights. Please keep in mind these are reported in percentages and should not be considered averages.

In the face of this full-force epidemic, there needs to be exercise for all Americans. For activity to be effective, it must go beyond the present sedentary lifestyles of most children and adults. A goal must be to reach 60 minutes of high-energy activity every day, seven days a week. That is a real challenge for almost every man, woman, and child in this country, requiring a major lifestyle change and commitment. Our lives have taken us in a direction almost void of simple physical activity. Our parents and grandparents moved more, walked more, and even played more. While their play may not have been intense, it was regular and consistent. Kids played with other kids as a neighborhood activity, not waiting for organized leagues. Current social and physical environments have made this less likely to occur for safety, logistical, or family reasons (such as no parent home after school). Somewhere along the way toward a growing prosperity, we lost the fundamentals of playtime. Sadder still, we have lost recess, physical education, and structured and unstructured physical activities in most of our nation's schools during the day. Furthermore, in the past decades, we have lost any real physical activity before and after school. Almost no one gets enough activity daily to avoid being caught in this weight gain trap. With no plan of action, weight gain and the associated medical problems are occurring at younger ages, and the medical problems are getting more complicated.

As a society, we are living longer than past generations, mostly due to modern antibiotics and sanitation advancements occurring in the last 60 years. The quality of that long life, though, is now being compromised by our wayward eating and activity habits as well as our emphasis on convenience and saving time. With this new culture emerging and the current weight epidemic expanding, we may be leaving a legacy of a shorter life span for future generations.

Economists have become keenly aware of the American obesity problem and many articles have been written

"In the face of this full-force epidemic, there needs to be exercise for all Americans. For activity to be effective, it must go beyond the present sedentary lifestyles of most children and adults. A goal must be to reach 60 minutes of high-energy activity every day, seven days a week. That is a real challenge for almost every man, woman, and child in this country, requiring a major lifestyle change and commitment."

from their perspective. At an event sponsored by the Economic Research Service, U.S. Department of Agriculture (2003), many interesting observations and conclusions were drawn about the American weight problem. What we, the authors, have learned about the economics of obesity has altered our approach to and understanding of the growing global epidemic. Economists in the government and private sector have emphasized the technological advances that have made work at home and in the office more sedentary and food prices lower through agricultural innovations. Physical activity has declined due to the shift to more sedentary occupations. Food intake has increased due to lower food prices, more availability, and 24-hour access. The explosion of women in the workforce has helped to create the demand for fast food chains, restaurants, convenience stores, and mass-produced foods that are now within easy travel distances for most Americans. The fast food industry has made buying a meal so convenient that there is a fast food location within a five-minute drive (or walk, in city living) for those residing in urban areas. Parents make food choices based on limited time and available income. A model presented at this meeting suggested that 40% of recent weight gain may be due to lower food prices and 60% due to decreased physical activity.

Though not intentionally, single women and mothers in the workplace have dramatically changed the eating patterns of both singles and families. A mother's employment may impact the likelihood of her child being overweight, and the number of hours a day a working mother is away from home predicts the probability of a child becoming overweight. The reduction in home time for mothers promotes children being fed less home-cooked meals and more fast food meals and convenience foods—most of which are high in fats and sugars. Eating fast food twice a week gives a person an 86% greater chance of becoming obese as compared with someone who eats fast food only once a week (Brownell & Horgen, 2004). Working mothers also appear to put much less emphasis on monitoring the exercise habits of their children.

Some Alarming Facts

Children of highly educated working mothers are significantly more likely to be overweight. African American and Hispanic children are significantly more likely to be overweight. This is further complicated by the level of the mother's education and other sociological factors beyond the scope of this book.

When someone else does the food preparation, such as when food is purchased from a restaurant or a fast food establishment or pre-made from the grocery store, content, quality, choice, and portions are much less monitored and less predictable. We have a tendency to eat the entire amount of prepared food we have purchased, even though we would have put less on our plate had we prepared it ourselves. People who are having trouble losing weight often underestimate their calorie consumption by as much as 50%.

The good news is that there are things that can be done, both to prevent and improve an unhealthy weight situation in an individual. We can't currently alter our genetic makeup, but we can make an impact on life issues. Fat storage can be turned into fat burning. The potential exists to change the perception and the role of food as well as the value of activity in our lives. Creating a healthier, longer, and better life quality means lowering the risk for the medical diseases so strongly associated with being at an unhealthy weight. As we age, we are increasingly at risk to store fat. Our muscle mass will decrease and our fat mass will increase, even if weight remains the same. A focus on good nutrition and exercise can play a role in preventing this shift.

Adults characteristically put on 25 pounds between the ages of 20 and 45. Some of us put on even more. With greater than 61% of adults being in the overweight or obese categories, those of us in society who have an influence on children and adolescents may be in a position to educate, encourage, and change the weight status of our youth and influence unhealthy adult weight gain. Knowledge is power, and prevention efforts at the school level must be an effective communal and societal exercise. We may have to work on improving ourselves to be able to influence others successfully: "When school personnel embrace health, they act as role models for healthful living" (Andersen et al., 2004). Scientific research will lead to more and better answers, but until that happens, we need to concentrate on reversing the factors over which we have control. We *do* have some control over what our children and adolescents eat and their lack of physical activity. We *can* provide our youth with reasons why they should be concerned and give them support and incentives to comply.

Societal pressures and the current environment make it difficult for adolescents to do it on their own, and our younger children cannot make these decisions in a vacuum. Your position as a significant authority figure outside the home puts you in a unique position to make an impact on this problem that affects a significant number of your students. The school day provides a fixed place and frequent contact where a focus on nutrition and physical activity change can have a large positive effect. Goals go beyond taking away unhealthy foods from the cafeteria and removing sugar drinks and most candies from the vending machines. Those actions do not effect change in personal habits, they just limit access. We must get into the heads of our children. Education leads to understanding and sets the groundwork for change, and positive lifestyle changes promote better health. A healthier child has a better opportunity to learn.

1.4. Unhealthy weight of students has a major negative impact on their personal health and wellness.

The negative impact of childhood obesity touches every aspect of a student's life.

The problems the childhood obesity epidemic creates for us are immense. There are far-reaching medical, personal, psychological, and social consequences that could begin prior to kindergarten. The health problems associated with overweight adults are now being seen in adolescents with greater frequency as the obesity epidemic expands. Weight-related health problems that are medically controlled in adults become more difficult to treat if they begin during childhood or adolescence. This may mean multiple medicines instead of a single drug. It could mean a higher dose of each drug. Multiple drugs and higher doses increase the cost of medications and can possibly lead to more drug side effects.

One out of every four severely overweight adolescents already has high blood pressure and is possibly taking a prescription medication. Diabetes of the adult type, called Type 2 diabetes, is now common in school-age children and not only carries with it all the problems of diabetes but also promotes the development of premature heart disease. High triglyceride fat and cholesterol are common, as is low HDL (this good cholesterol should be high), as weight increases in children. Most of these problems can be prevented or partially reversed by weight control and with increased physical activity. Childhood asthma symptoms decrease with weight loss. In addition to medical problems associated with increased weight, low self-esteem and feelings of decreased personal worth may begin to emerge. We will discuss these issues in later chapters.

With 80% of severely overweight adolescents becoming obese adults, the logic of working to prevent this disease in children is compelling. Dr. Dietz reports that by the time overweight children are of school age, unhealthy weight should be addressed (Dietz, Bland, Gortmaker, Molloy, & Schmid, 2002). Intervention at an early stage in the evolution of obesity makes success more likely and complications less frequent or easier to treat medically or psychologically.

Figure 1.1   Prevalence of Overweight Among Children and
Adolescents Ages 6–19 Years

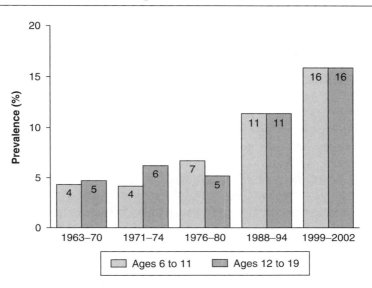

SOURCE: National Center for Health Statistics (n.d.); data from CDC/NCHS, NHES, and NHANES.

According to the Center for Health and Health Care in Schools (2003), overweight in childhood has more than doubled, and in adolescents has tripled, in the last 20 years.

Young Hispanics and African Americans have the highest rates of being at an unhealthy weight or obese. Older girls have a greater problem than boys, and of males, Hispanic boys are at the highest risk. Unless enlightened and innovative decision makers take a role in stemming the tide, the situation for our children will deteriorate further. The bottom line for educators is that all children come together in the melting pot of the school day. While the youth of America are not without personal responsibilities here, a direction to change must be afforded to them in a manner they understand so they can see the value and have ownership in the process. Recognition for participating is an incentive. Educators becoming aware of changes in weight and BMI will help identify the at-risk, overweight, or obese children who themselves may not be aware of their situation. Adolescent boys in particular can be unaware of being overweight, especially if they are comparing themselves to more seriously overweight family members. Monitoring will track the more recalcitrant youngsters and allow for more time to be spent with those with greater needs. This monitoring is not the role of educators, but the identification process may open the door for parents and health care providers to intervene.

Pediatric medical literature is full of information linking parental involvement as one of the best predictors of short-term and long-term weight control in children ages 8 to 12 years. How parents approach making changes in how, when, and what the family eats and how individual parents address their children's eating habits vary greatly. The most well-meaning parent can cause conflict with their children and the habits they wish to change by misrepresenting their motives to their kids. Parents have both the right and the obligation to see to the health of their children and to control the degree of lifestyle change a family will make. Schools progressive enough to identify unhealthy-weight students could possibly channel families to the right kind of help in the community. This usually means asking a pediatrician for advice. This approach may help reinforce healthier attitudes and better compliance with eating issues and physical activity at home.

Nutrition issues are now centered on food choices, portion size, snacking, and the amounts of fruits and vegetables consumed in an effort to achieve a healthy weight and provide optimum nutrition. Children's eating habits have always been the concern of parents, doctors, and educators. Past efforts, however, were centered on providing enough food for survival, health, and being able to work. Those meals were usually cooked fresh and eaten at home, and most contained a high percentage of vegetables and fruit.

In our current living environment, nearly two-thirds of school-age children and adolescents are living with a single and employed parent or two working parents; for this modern busy family, "convenience rules." Ease of food preparation, time, and cost considerations loom large. Restraints of time, money, and convenience easily lead to many unhealthy food options. Technology has provided a faster life and a fatter body for adults and has helped create the same weight problem in our children. High-quality foods are usually more expensive than high-fat, calorie-dense foods and usually take more preparation time. This adds to the problem families have living on a tight budget and a limited schedule and contributes to the high percentage of unhealthy weight among the lowest income groups.

Of all foods, high-fat and high-calorie items are the easiest to obtain. They take the least amount of time out of a busy day to buy or prepare. Fast food restaurants are everywhere, and many of those foods are readily available 24 hours a day. Convenience stores are another outlet for fast foods and snack foods, as are vending machines, grocery stores, school cafeterias, and school drink/snack machines.

Today's parents don't cook as often as their parents did. Some families eat most of their meals outside the home. When the only reference point to portion size is a restaurant plate, a Chinese takeout portion, a super-sized fast food meal, or a pizza pie, a distorted view of a true portion size is created. The average restaurant main course, for example, if nonfried, without gravy or breading on meat or fish, and with steamed or fresh vegetables, is equal to about 1000 calories. To lose weight, consuming somewhere between 1000 and 2500 calories for the entire day is usually in order. The problem is further compounded by parents if they do not elect to send lunch to school for their children. By recent legal changes in most states, only healthy foods will be made available for children at lunch, but until that becomes universal, the cafeteria is a source of food choices that undermine the healthy needs of our students. Furthermore, meals that include fruits and vegetables likely decrease the health risks of many chronic diseases.

Insufficient consumption of fruits and vegetables is a big problem in adults and in our school-age population. The average woman eats one to two vegetables a day, and a man has one to none. With adults as the model for our children, the chances are small that they could possibly eat better without parental changes. The recommended servings of fruits and vegetables are five a day, and only 25% of adolescents and 20% of all school-age children meet this goal. Adding appropriate amounts of fruits and vegetables to a child's diet will help prevent or improve an overweight situation. The reasons may be that fruits and vegetables are filling and satisfying and there can be a decrease in total calories consumed. This would also mean that some of the more calorie-dense foods and snacks have been decreased in daily eating.

Figure 1.2   New Food Pyramid

SOURCE: U.S. Department of Agriculture.

Only about 20% of school kids eat balanced meals, even in the school cafeteria. Milk drinking is down, and pediatricians now worry about the bone health of children and adolescents. A soft drink a day is not unusual for school kids, and one-third of teenagers average three soft drinks a day. At this rate, our children have little chance to develop good, healthy eating attitudes, to consume healthy balanced meals, and to enjoy good health through life. It is possible that in some unhealthy-eating households, a student's only semblance of a balanced meal is at school.

Eating habits are learned mostly, at home from family norms and social environments. Through the thousands of food advertisements a year seen by our TV-watching children, an interest in eating more unhealthy snacks, fast foods, and sweetened drinks has increased. If not educated on the subject, children and adolescents may not even know they are eating themselves to ill health and an unhealthy weight. Many parents are not in a position to teach their children what they themselves don't even know.

The fattening of America is partly a matter of ignorance and misconceptions, both of which are correctable. We are not stupid, just without the knowledge base we need. Although many

Figure 1.3 Pyramid Information

GRAINS	VEGETABLES	FRUITS	MILK	MEAT & BEANS
Make half your grains whole	Vary your veggies	Focus on fruits	Get your calcium-rich foods	Go lean with protein
Eat at least 3 oz. of whole-grain cereals, breads, crackers, rice, or pasta every day	Eat more dark-green veggies like broccoli, spinach, and other dark leafy greens	Eat a variety of fruit	Go low-fat or fat-free when you choose milk, yogurt, and other milk products	Choose low-fat or lean meats and poultry
1 oz. is about 1 slice of bread, about 1 cup of breakfast cereal, or ½ cup of cooked rice, cereal, or pasta	Eat more orange vegetables like carrots and sweet potatoes Eat more dry beans and peas like pinto beans, kidney beans, and lentils	Choose fresh, frozen, canned, or dried fruit Go easy on fruit juices	If you don't or can't consume milk, choose lactose-free products or other calcium sources such as fortified foods and beverages	Bake it, broil it, or grill it Vary your protein routine – choose more fish, beans, peas, nuts, and seeds

For a 2,000-calorie diet, you need the amounts below from each food group. To find the amounts that are right for you, go to MyPyramid.gov.

Eat 6 oz. every day	Eat 2½ cups every day	Eat 2 cups every day	Get 3 cups every day; for kids aged 2 to 8, it's 2	Eat 5½ oz. every day

Find your balance between food and physical activity
- Be sure to stay within your daily calorie needs.
- Be physically active for at least 30 minutes most days of the week.
- About 60 minutes a day of physical activity may be needed to prevent weight gain.
- For sustaining weight loss, at least 60 to 90 minutes a day of physical activity may be required.
- Children and teenagers should be physically active for 60 minutes every day, or most days.

Know the limits on fats, sugars, and salt (sodium)
- Make most of your fat sources from fish, nuts, and vegetable oils.
- Limit solid fats like butter, stick margarine, shortening, and lard, as well as foods that contain these.
- Check the Nutrition Facts label to keep saturated fats, trans fats, and sodium low.
- Choose food and beverages low in added sugars. Added sugars contribute calories with few, if any, nutrients.

MyPyramid.gov
STEPS TO A HEALTHIER YOU

USDA

U.S. Department of Agriculture
Center for Nutrition Policy and Promotion
April 2005
CNPP-15

USDA is an equal opportunity provider and employer.

teachers may have been educated in the area of nutrition, it may not be sufficient to fill this knowledge gap in parents and children. Doctors don't even have a full grasp of the situation, and they have the responsibility of dealing with the consequences of being overweight. In reality, teachers also deal with some of the negative consequences children have when overweight, so there is reason to do what is practical to prevent and minimize these consequences.

According to the CDC, there are more medications prescribed, more physician visits required, and more frequent hospitalizations needed due to poor exercise habits in kids. Lack of physical activity is related to direct medical costs totaling $76 billion in the year 2000.

American children simply do not exercise, and neither do their parents. About 61.5% of children do not participate in any organized physical activity during nonschool hours, and 22.6% do not engage in any free-time physical activity. The policy statement from the American Academy of Pediatrics, "Prevention of Pediatric Overweight and Obesity," reviews national survey data and indicates that 20% of U.S. children reported two or fewer vigorous physical activity sessions per week, and more than 25% watched at least four hours of television per day. The heavier children watched more TV than average-weight children by 50%. African American and Hispanic children are significantly less likely than Caucasian children to report involvement in organized exercise activities. Low income and the education levels of these parents are additional factors.

1.5. Unhealthy weight impacts the academic achievement and emotional-social development of students.

The effect of unhealthy weight on academic achievement is not clear. What does occur is a loss of continuity of learning through missed school days due to illness associated with being overweight. Other issues are social and psychological ones that interfere with learning, such as a lack of self-confidence, teacher prejudice, peer discrimination, and nonacceptance into the group.

A Case Study

One such example is that of an overweight student who showed poor classroom participation and who answered meekly when called upon in class. His attitude in class was misunderstood by one of his teachers, who accused the student of having outside help with his homework and project scores since they were consistently excellent. His lack of expression in class, however, was a reflection of poor self-confidence and self-image, not academic acuity. He did well on class examinations. This student found a mentor in a teacher who understood his image issues and helped him realize he had things to contribute. This same student could have been a poor overall student were it not for a concerned teacher.

Unhealthy eating undermines expected growth and cognitive function development. Unhealthy weight promotes the development of many chronic diseases we have already discussed and weakens body response to infection.

Since a significant percentage of our youth are either at an unhealthy weight or at risk for it, everything points to attempting innovative, aggressive prevention measures. In a study conducted by the California Department of Education, Delaine Eastin, State Superintendent of Public Instruction, reported a positive relationship between academic achievement and the physical fitness of California public school students. Results were based on matching mathematics and reading scores from the spring 2001 state achievement test with a mandated physical fitness test of 600,000 students in Grades 5, 7, and 9. Higher levels of achievement were associated with higher levels of fitness at each of the three grade levels (2002). Dr. Eastin feels that there is proof available that children learn more when physically fit. Teachers overwhelmingly appreciate the relationship between being physically active and having a better ability to learn (Robert Wood Johnson Foundation, 2003). It has been widely accepted that relationships exist between good physical fitness and positive self-esteem and lower negative effects of unchecked stress.

In a later study conducted in Chicago, a wellness approach in instruction used one hour a day of stretching yoga and good nutrition. The Namaste School principal, Allison Slade, stated that the K–1 program is working great. The approach is to integrate health instruction, practice good nutrition, and focus on physical fitness to increase academic achievement—and they are getting great results (personal communication, May 8, 2005). The school is located on Chicago's southwest side. In *The Learning Connection: Value of Improving Nutrition and Physical Activity in Our Schools* (Satcher, n.d.), the author in this report estimated that well-nourished students tend to be better students, while poorly nourished ones have weaker academic performance and score lower on standardized achievement tests. Lower math scores and likelihood of repeating a grade were also reported.

An interesting point for all principals to consider is if students miss meals, their cognitive development and school performance can be negatively affected. Increased participation in the nation's School Breakfast Program has been associated with increased academic test scores, daily attendance, and class participation. It has also been linked to reductions in tardiness and absenteeism. These same students are reported by teachers and parents to be calmer in class and to have more energy to study, according to Dr. Satcher, the former surgeon general of the United States and founder of Action for Healthy Kids, a national initiative addressing the obesity epidemic.

We cannot emphasize enough: *American children simply do not exercise, and neither do their parents.* Physical education at schools has been seriously compromised in recent years, and there is little exemplary exercise behavior demonstrated on the part of teachers for their own good or as role models for students.

In a brief interview with Dr. Satcher in Orlando after his address to the attendees at the Annual Conference of the Association of Supervision and Curriculum Development, Dr. Queen had the opportunity to talk with Dr. Satcher about the growing epidemic. Responding to the question of what we must do, he stated that it will take "multi-

> "American children simply do not exercise, and neither do their parents."

ple partnerships between the medical and educational professions," in addition to other organizations, to significantly slow the process of childhood obesity and the related consequences (personal correspondence, April 4, 2005).

Parents have always told children, "To be strong and healthy and to do well at school, you must start your day with a healthy breakfast. To have energy, to be able to concentrate in class, and to compete in sports, you must not skip meals, and you may only have a snack or dessert if you finish your meal." There is now scientific evidence behind these intuitive truths, and the documented relationship between performance and proper eating is growing; this is also true in students who participate in the School Breakfast Program. Dr. Satcher (1995) quickly shared and promoted strongly in the organization he founded, Action for Kids, that an increase in test scores, daily attendance, and class participation has been reported by educators teaching in schools with the School Breakfast Program. Furthermore, tardiness and absenteeism appears to have been reduced (Tufts University School of Nutrition, 1995).

CHAPTER TWO

The Principal's Role as an Agent of Change

School leaders would be wise to consider enacting programs to combat physical inactivity, poor nutrition, and over-weight and obesity among school staff, especially teachers and principals who serve as role models for students. Such programs will not only lead to better nutrition and improved physical activity among students who emulate their teacher's behaviors, they can also reduce expenses and lead to higher-quality instruction.

—Action for Healthy Kids, 2004, p. 20

Critical Question 2

As the school principal, what is my role as an
agent of change in prevention and education in this
epidemic of overweight and obese students?

THE ESSENTIAL TRUTHS

2.1. As the instructional leader, you are responsible for guiding and developing the school's vision for overall student success.

2.2. Within your role in the implementation of the required federal, state, and district standards, one specific task is to provide the leadership in integrating a program for the prevention and education of overweight and obese students within the existing curriculum.

2.3. As an instructional leader, you must serve as a healthy role model to teachers, staff, students, parents, and members of the community. Healthy role modeling is about making changes.

2.4. As principal, you must ensure each student has a qualified teacher and provide a comprehensive professional growth plan for each faculty member that includes a personal healthy weight and wellness component so that he or she can serve as an appropriate role model to students.

2.5. As the leader for the staff development of teachers in your school, you must provide training opportunities for faculty to learn concepts in health and wellness, in addition to instructional techniques for implementing integrated instruction within the classroom.

2.6. With direct input from powerful special interest groups, professional organizations, and the food and beverage industry, you must be proactive in implementing a successful program for overweight and obese students. As the school principal, you must develop partnerships with civic organizations, local businesses, medical professionals, and the media to obtain the necessary human and financial resources needed to support the implementation of the above program.

Failure to implement an effective program will result in greater input and control from outside agencies.

2.7. The school principal provides a safe and orderly environment to confront and resolve negative issues impacting the overall growth and academic achievement of all students, including those who are overweight and obese.

PRACTICAL GUIDES TO THE ESSENTIAL TRUTHS

2.1. As the instructional leader, you are responsible for guiding and developing the school's vision for overall student success.

Superintendents and principals readily understand the roles needed for their positions. Today, with the standards movement of the new century, educational leaders have the pressures of attempting to lead schools and districts in an attempt to meet societal demands to increase student achievement; respond to diverse populations; and balance numerous roles as instructional leaders, community activists, and school managers. With respect to the principal, much of the research has focused on the "undoability" of the position in the current highly political climate. So much attention on educational leadership has been focused on increasing test scores, especially with at-risk students, that by far the majority of the school day is directed to that end, bringing teachers, staff, and students to practice for what may be artificial gains in achievement and not real, sustained learning. During the process, the principal may be leading many stakeholders in the school to higher levels of stress and unhealthy work conditions, which may be contributing to what Queen and Queen (2005) refer to as "schools as a culture of stress" (p. 1).

What if we could show educational leaders how to significantly increase student achievement; save millions of dollars in student expenditures; improve the health and wellness of principals, teachers, and staff; and, most important, save the lives of millions of K–12 students . . . would you be interested? Of course you would, as would all dedicated leaders or teachers as well as parents and concerned citizens for the overall success of America's children and youth!

2.2. Within your role in the implementation of the required federal, state, and district standards, one specific task is to provide the leadership in integrating a program for the prevention and education of overweight and obese students within the existing curriculum.

In our respective roles, we, the authors of this text, are often labeled as visionaries by our peers. What we collectively see rapidly approaching is the demand for the school leaders of America to add the responsibility to their already overworked schedules of becoming voices in preventing and decreasing the childhood obesity epidemic. Basically, it has become a major issue in the past few years, and while there is always much talk about community partnerships and teaming with organizations, we must face what history has expected of education: to be the panacea or cure-all for the ills of society. If anything was ever an ill of society, the childhood obesity epidemic is it.

As a caveat, historically, Colin Greer (1973) reminds us in *The Great School Legend* of the claim that the school system takes students from a diversity of backgrounds and of varying abilities and molds them into a productive middle class—the pride of America. As Greer informs the reader, the "great school legend" was historically the main reason for the lack of change in schools to meet societal needs. While we will always have individuals preaching that schools should not take on certain tasks, we believe that in the current American sociopolitical climate, the public school system is by far the best vehicle in the best situation to solve the growing epidemic of childhood obesity in society . . . and it is perhaps the only major nationwide institution where specific concepts and outcomes will be taught, measured, and validated.

> "The public school system is by far the best vehicle in the best situation to solve the growing epidemic of childhood obesity in society."

As a physician and educator, we have teamed to guide you, the educational leader, in how to make curricular and instructional changes that can significantly prevent or decrease the rate of childhood obesity while improving student wellness, increasing academic achievement, and promoting partnerships.

You may be surprised to know that one of the early curricula in America was known as the *Seven Cardinal Principles*, written in 1918. These cardinal principles were intended learning outcomes that students in the schools should achieve. The *Seven Cardinal Principles* was written to prepare public school students to live in post–World War I America in the following areas: health, command of fundamental processes, worthy home membership, vocation, citizenship, worthy use of leisure time, and ethical character (Tanner & Tanner, 2007). Perhaps now is the time to add the Eighth Cardinal Principle for America's schools: preventing childhood obesity.

If the members of the committee that introduced the seven cardinal principles were living today, they would surely agree with us that the eighth principle would be a major curricular focus on the prevention of childhood obesity in today's schools. In the remaining sections of the text, we will present detailed information and tools to achieve this principle. The intention of our approach is to provide you, the principal or school leader, with information to save you time and to help you assist your teachers, and, ultimately, the children in preventing and perhaps even reversing this deadly epidemic.

As a school leader, you learned quickly that principals are held responsible for every aspect of the school, including the building, teacher development, curriculum implementation, and the academic achievement of students, to list just a few. More important, we know as educators that our decisions and actions greatly impact students physically, emotionally, socially, medically, and academically, not only during the formative years of schooling but well into their adult years. Such is the power of an educator.

> "Perhaps now is the time to add the Eighth Cardinal Principle for America's schools: preventing childhood obesity."

Since the 1980s, researchers have placed a primary focus on changing roles in principal leadership. In the last 20 years, both the public and principals have demonstrated major concern about the evolving role of the principalship. These changes have resulted from the increased demands of state and federal agencies. The No Child Left Behind Act of 2001 is a great example. Principals have been a focus of federal and state standards, high-stakes testing, and accountability. Principals are working an average of 70-plus hours a week. Schools have changed the roles of principals with regard to the school day. Principals are responsible for all the activities within the school environment, regardless of when the day starts or ends. Tirozzi, executive director of the National Association of Secondary School Principals, and Ferrandino, executive director of the National Association of Elementary School Principals, summarized the problem of the increasing diversity and complexity of principals' roles when they stated the following:

> The principal must be a legal expert, health and social services coordinator, fundraiser, public relations consultant, security officer, who is technologically savvy, diplomatic with top-notch managerial skills, whose most important duty is the implementation of instructional programs, curricula, pedagogical practice, and assessment models. (Tirozzi & Ferrandino, 2001, p. 14)

We believe that the principal's roles and responsibilities will increase yet again with the added responsibility of ensuring that health and wellness are included within the school curriculum with limited resources.

Historically, schools have been held accountable for many of the ills of society, and within the same mode, schools are viewed as the societal vehicle or panacea to resolve the particular issue. Many issues facing schools have been within the realm of possible resolution and thus appropriate for schools to undertake, yet it is true that many others are far beyond the scope of what the school should be even attempting to address. With that said, however, we do believe the principal must have the vision to guide the school in the direction that responds to many of the issues facing society today and in the future.

Principals and teachers are in the best situation to deal with many issues facing our society today. Within the structure of the educational system, the roles of the principal, teacher, and support personnel are usually clearly defined. In each school, we find excellent educators capable of performing well in their defined roles. While we agree that most of these issues should be addressed by other agencies within our society, the school system already has the expertise and many of the tools to deal with the overweight and obese student. Unfortunately, this expertise has not been identified. More specifically, the classroom teacher has not been given the opportunity to directly address or teach concepts dealing with overall student wellness. From our perspective, both medically and educationally, principals must ensure that teachers are provided the opportunity to address this delicate issue. Furthermore, it is the principal's responsibility to expand the vision to ensure teachers receive the necessary staff development and instructional materials to integrate the content of student wellness within the framework of the existing instructional program. Integrating different content within existing lessons is nothing new to the classroom teacher. A good staff development program will build on the lifelong knowledge of health and wellness that all educators have practiced all their lives in one form or another.

2.3. As an instructional leader, you must serve as a healthy role model to teachers, staff, students, parents, and members of the community. Healthy role modeling is about making changes.

In our opinion, the first role of the principal is to serve as a model to faculty, staff, and students. Achieving a healthy weight is first about making changes. To be successful, you must choose to change for the right reasons. Your reasons could be many, but similar to reading a food label, the first two listed ingredients tell you if you have made the correct healthy choice. Metaphorically, the first two ingredients for improving your health are choosing to lose weight and developing an approach using small changes. Celebrate the preparations to be ready for the starting day. You must choose to be both psychologically and functionally ready. It will be a day to celebrate the beginning of a new you.

Choose what behavior to initially change. Pick a battle you can win and accomplish in a reasonably short period of time. A victory over an easy

> "To be successful, you must choose to change for the right reasons."

behavior needing change will be a driving force and give you confidence to then choose other more difficult challenges. For example, make a decision to drink six to eight glasses of water each day. The more difficult the change, the more time you should allow for that habit to be altered.

Habits may develop quickly or slowly, but changing them is never fast. There is always the honeymoon period in which it seems easy to make a transition from a bad habit to a better one, only to find that you are slipping back into old habits. It is all a learning experience; you must take a setback for what it is, a momentary lapse, a reminder that perseverance will eventually conquer. The stimulus to eat is a natural survival mechanism. What you must choose is to change your eating habits, not to deprive and starve yourself. You must relearn to eat in a healthier manner. Plan on eating three meals each day and eat on a time schedule . . . not on a when-I'm-hungry schedule. Choose a day, choose a time, make an appointment with yourself, and keep it.

When you identify what to change, begin simply, even if it is a major change. Stopping or decreasing your snack consumption, or eliminating breakfast at a fast food place or a coffee shop, may be harder habits to tackle. Maybe your choice can be to pick two or three days a week when you will have a bowl of high-fiber cereal and skim milk plus a piece of fruit as your breakfast. It should not take any longer to eat at home then it takes to wait in the takeout line. Planning is the challenge. It may be easier to protect yourself against lunchtime eating mistakes by carrying your lunch several days a week. This is another planning challenge. Each day that lunch is carried is a victory.

You may wish to start by increasing your activity level but that may not be the most important way to begin. Your best starting point on the road to healthy weight is to focus on cutting back on your food intake. Let exercise come at a later stage. You will probably get a better jumpstart on your weight loss goal with an initial action focused on food choices and portion size. Exercise is important but is not the defining issue in your mission to lose weight. Exercise is, however, a marker of the person who will sustain weight loss.

When choosing snacks, think healthy—fruit or air-popped popcorn are tasty choices. Choices from the vending machine in the teacher's lounge should be water or diet drinks. A goal at school is to stay away from junk foods. The risk is also at home. The more junk foods you keep in the house, the more vulnerable you become. If these snacks are for you, then try to be disciplined and stop buying them. If they are for someone else, you need to rethink how necessary it is to have them in the house. No one needs junk foods on demand. But if these foods must be in the house, do not keep them in a highly visible location. You will be less tempted if you can't see them. Be patient with your progress. Weight gain did not occur overnight and will take time to reverse, so choose to stick with your plan.

Setting *personal goals* is critical in making lifestyle changes. Goals force you to plan the structure that will help you accomplish that goal. Goals give you direction, something to work toward over time. Goals allow you to focus on the changes that are most important to get you there, and they provide a measure by which you can gauge your progress. When you accomplish a goal, your next planned challenge may become clearer to you, since you now have a different perspective on your progress. Choosing realistic goals gives you reasonable assurances that your efforts will be successful. Take your time and choose well at the beginning of your journey to better health and weight.

Not all plans turn out to be practical, so be prepared to go in a different direction if need be. Remember to take pleasure in every small step and every little success because these add up as progress. You need to take credit and affirm yourself each time you succeed in making a personal change. Write these down and watch your successes accumulate.

When writing your goals, include reasons why you want to achieve them. This keeps your motivation clearly in front of you as a reminder and a source of encouragement. Include when you will begin working on these goals and how you will initiate them. Focus your goals on those things within your power to change.

> "There will be many battles on the way to healthy weight.
> You must choose to win each, one at a time."

Realize that you may need help to attain some of your harder goals. Be thinking about where that help may come from.

You *need an attitude.* There will be many battles on the way to healthy weight. You must choose to win each, one at a time. *Life experiences have taught you that no one wins all the time.* Sometimes a victory means preventing a bad habit from getting worse. The all-or-nothing attitude should not be your attitude. Win some, lose some—it is part of life. The most successful people know that winning means exposing yourself to losing. In the weight control arena, everything is a relearning experience, including confronting a setback. A setback is a lapse. You must learn to recognize a lapse. An example is slipping back into the habit of stopping off for fast food, including fries and a soft drink, maybe even dessert, on the way home when you have had a late day at school or a late meeting. This can be corrected by having available a frozen low-fat meal in the freezer at home, giving you an alternative to stopping for fast food and thus getting you out of a lapse mode. It is easy to recover from a lapse if you train yourself to recognize it for what it is—a reversion to old habits or just getting lazy. If you do not know you have lapsed—you have relapsed. A relapse can trigger giving up. Do not give up. You can recover from a relapse. It takes more work and you may need some help, but it is definitely doable. Weight gain did not occur overnight and will take time to reverse, so choose to stick with your plan. In your plan, you must make room to include more activity in your busy week. We will talk about this later.

The *process of change* can be feared and resisted or embraced as an adventure. Emotional, intellectual, and spiritual growth is a continuing journey involving many changes. Permanent weight loss occurs when you are motivated to make lifestyle changes. Failure happens only when you stop trying. Be ready to change, be ready to succeed, and be ready to make mistakes. Use a mistake as a learning tool rather than a sign of failure. For example, if you are exercising and were planning to take a walk in the neighborhood as soon as you got home but went to the mall instead, replay that event in your mind. What was so important at the mall? If it was important to be there, then you should have planned to walk through the mall for another 30 minutes after you made your purchase to attain your exercise goal. (Don't forget to change your shoes into more comfortable ones before walking.)

Self-monitoring change is important for your progress. It is comparable to the value of homework and test scores to gauge student progress. Confirmation is important. When you succeed, appreciate it, applaud it, and congratulate yourself. Do not, however, criticize falling short of your goal. It is easier to slip than it is to succeed. There will always be another meal, another time for exercise, another day. But do not hesitate in getting back on track. Do not let your weight loss plans be stopped or misdirected by a lapse. Learn from a lapse how to prevent the next one in a similar situation. Only you can stop yourself.

Self-monitoring may mean keeping an occasional food and activity diary. We all remember what we ate today and maybe yesterday, but the day before yesterday is often a blur. A food diary will do one of two things for you. You may record everything you eat and see how well you did and then make changes as necessary. However, with the process of writing down your choices, portions, and when you ate, you may be inclined to make changes on the spot. The same can be said for an exercise diary. Both are good tools and are means of positive learning reinforcement.

You need to *enforce lifestyle decisions.* Do you have a structured life schedule? Do you eat three meals a day and eat on time? Do you have school and business meal obligations or eat often with colleagues or eat out with family and friends? Did you choose water to drink from the faculty soda machine? Do you know what you will you do to increase your physical activity? Will you make exercise a regular part of your week and not let it get usurped by other obligations? Are you ready to make a commitment for the long haul? Do you have a support group in place? If the answers to these questions are no, you are not doomed, but you will need to decide if you are ready and willing to reestablish control of your life. Your weight may be the only facet of your life over which you do not feel in control. If the answer to some of the questions is yes, then you are ahead of the game. Life schedules may not be totally changeable, but what is? Preparing food (even with minimal cooking) and eating three meals a day are doable acts. Exercise can become part of your plan as well.

> "Be ready to change, be ready to succeed, and be ready to make mistakes."

Without structure, you can be doomed in the process. You exist in a structured profession. The structure to control weight must fit your lifestyle. For example, if you skip breakfast, ask yourself why. The answer probably is that you are not hungry, or you lack time, or you believe that if you eat in the morning, you will eat too much at lunch. You may even feel that you don't need those morning calories. All of these objections are answerable when you realize that healthy calories in the morning will help get you started, stoking your fire, so to speak, and prevent low energy, low blood sugar, and the resultant hunger later in the day.

What if lunch is your problem? Are you someone who eats on the run or whose lunch is a spontaneous decision? Do you eat alone or with colleagues? How about food at your desk at noon or at 2:30 in the afternoon? Lunches can be planned in advance. (On the weekend, eating in a restaurant or even a fast food place can be planned to suit your calorie needs.)

Do you remember bringing brown bag lunches to school as a student? Why not try carrying lunch to provide a good example to your staff and students? Packing your own food is a good way to make healthy choices available. Packing your own lunch allows you to stay away from tempting foods and vending machines and is a great way to use leftovers. To be successful in carrying your lunch, you must have lunch-type foods readily available at home. This means grocery shopping using a shopping list. Do not go on a searching-for-lunch food mission without a list; be a designated shopper. Shopping for healthy meals is dangerous without the protection of a list.

Remember, whatever you choose to do, make it practical. Do not make promises to yourself you can't keep. This pertains to both nutritional changes and activity changes.

Remember to *eat at scheduled times*. Do not skip meals or go for long periods without eating. Your body is biologically and physiologically programmed for scheduled eating. When your body gets food at regular times, it burns calories more efficiently. On the other hand, long periods without food can push your body into a starvation mode. This means you could burn fewer calories and convert energy into body fat stores. When calorie deprived, your body may try to play catch-up, and you may find yourself overeating later in the day or even into the next day.

> "Do not skip meals or go for long periods without eating. When your body gets food at regular times, it burns calories more efficiently."

Eating before bedtime makes it hard to lose weight because your body is in a calorie shutdown mode at that time of day. If you are someone who gets up at night and eats, your calorie burning is compromised. Nighttime eating is a specific overweight eating disorder, as are binge eating and compulsive eating. These issues may need special medical attention to prevent you from becoming your own saboteur.

Remember that your body runs more efficiently if it has energy (food) during times of the day when body activity is high. When activity is low, the body needs less energy. All calories not used are stored. Sedentary activities burn very little energy. Inactivity can trigger a desire to eat, especially if meal skipping occurs at the same time.

Some people have an eating disorder. A binge eater is one who overeats a lot more than usual in a two-hour time period more often than three times a week for longer than three months. Compulsive and stress eaters have some characteristics in common. They are people who eat when anxious, sad, mad, or stressed, and they may feel guilty or angry with themselves about it. Other individuals have a nighttime eating disorder and eat if they wake up during the night. You need to think about these disorders and seek professional help if you suspect you suffer from one of the above disorders.

Be aware of the following dietary facts! Adults and children in America eat almost no fruits and vegetables each day. These nutrients contain some of the lowest calories and the highest bulk per serving. They provide fiber, vitamins, minerals, and water content, as well as antioxidants and phytochemicals to fight cancer. You can find fresh, frozen, or canned vegetables to add to your meals. Want to be more satisfied and full at the end of your meal and eat less total calories at the same time? Add vegetables to your lunch or dinner meal. You may be overdoing fast food. Do you know that 35% to 40% of the average family food budget is spent on fast food? Be sure you do not fit into this statistic. Soft drinks provide only sugar calories. A 12-ounce can of soda has nine teaspoons of sugar, and children consume 11% of their daily caloric intake from soft drinks. Some of these are purchased from the school drink machines or at a school-sponsored event. Can you control what is sold at school-sponsored events?

Focus on calories. Focus on choices. Focus on portion control. Don't skip meals. Your goal is to accomplish all of the above. If you are inclined to start with a single focus and then progress, *there are no medically sound guidelines to help you.* There are, however, many views suggesting what is best. In our opinion, you may wish to initially focus on portion control.

Portion control is calorie control. Portion control is a learned phenomenon. It is based on calorie need, habit, genetics, hormones, enzymes, brain chemicals, and the total amount of food by weight that you consume. In our modern society, we have a distorted view of portion sizes. Because we eat out so often, we are fooled into believing that a restaurant serving or fast food order is portion correct. We could not be more wrong. Too much of any food can add weight to your frame. There are even plenty of vegetarians who are overweight. Portion size is especially challenging to those who eat out often.

Choices affect calories and affect the balancing of protein, carbohydrates, and fat in your meals. The more choices you have at a restaurant, especially if a buffet, the more portion mistakes and choice mistakes you could make. A distorted

> Learn to avoid portion distortion.

view of a true portion prevails, especially in a sit-down restaurant. Your best defense is to consider choosing your food before going to a restaurant. Will it be chicken or fish? Will it be baked or fried? Will I choose a six- or maybe a nine-ounce piece of meat with vegetables and no fries? If a baked potato is included, will I eat it all or half, and how much butter will I use? Will I be willing to hold the sour cream and bacon bits? If a salad starts the meal, will it have a creamy dressing, a low fat dressing or dressing on the side?

Remember that a majority of individuals who try but can't seem to lose weight readily underestimate their calorie intake by as much as 50%. Did you know that a coffee shop breakfast muffin could be two to three USDA (U.S. Department of Agriculture) servings, all wrapped into one muffin?

Put your fork down and take a drink of water between bites. We grew up learning to clean our plate; now learn to leave some food behind. Plan your meals ahead of time whenever possible. Take only a single portion when at home and when eating at someone's house, and try not to go back for seconds. If you are still hungry when your plate is empty, wait at least five minutes before thinking about an extra helping. Drink a glass of water before you eat. When at home, eat at the table, not in front of the TV or while reading. While you are eating, do nothing else except enjoy the company of others. Don't rush your meal. Take time to enjoy what you are eating. Taste each bite. This gives your brain the message that you are eating and allows your fullness mechanism time to give the cues that you are full and finished eating. Leave the table as soon as you are finished.

Because no one has superpowers, following a diet plan means having plenty of willpower; however, *willpower waxes and wanes.* The problem is that we continue to surround ourselves with foods and life situations that tempt us to make poor choices; the poor choices then lead to a feeling of personal weakness or lack of willpower. In truth, we are our own worst enemies when it comes to eating or not exercising. We set ourselves up to fail. To protect yourself, it makes sense to stay away from foods that make you vulnerable. If these foods never make it into your house, car, pocket, purse, or desk drawer, you can stay away from those temptations. This also applies to eating out. If you continue to go to your favorite restaurants where you tend to eat the wrong foods, it will be extremely difficult to avoid ordering unhealthy foods. One solution is to try restaurants where the menu is better suited to healthier choices.

Here are some other suggestions to reinforce your willpower: Never go grocery shopping when you are hungry. Always go to the grocery store with that list we have mentioned. Avoid buying too many of the non-nutritious foods that you like. At home, keep healthy foods in sight. Find some new healthy recipes to share with the family. Put leftovers in individual portions for the next day's packed lunch or freeze it for your own quick dinner meal.

You may need to divide a single plan into several sections. If attempting to eat three healthy meals a day is overwhelming to you, then break it down by focusing on making individual meals healthier. Start by planning one meal a day and choose the easiest meal with which to make that change. Focus on planning, shopping, and preparation for just that meal. When you are comfortable with your new routine, strategize ways to tackle your second meal.

This same technique can be used for initiating the exercise part of your weight management plan. Maybe you can begin by walking two or three days a week and then increase to four or five times. Later, concentrate on increasing your time spent walking and ultimately increase your walking speed. A reasonable initial exercise time is 15 to 20 minutes a session. Have your walking clothes and shoes ready and easily accessible. *Allow no excuse for avoiding that walk.* Dress appropriately if you are outside for this activity. Layer your clothes if the weather could change.

The most important initial *exercise goal* is how often you do it, the frequency. The second goal should be the amount of time spent exercising, followed by the third goal, adding intensity to your exercise program. The hardest part of your exercise program may be getting started. As a time saver, you may want to begin by walking around the school grounds before getting into your car to go home. Hint: Keep a change of shoes in your car.

Exercise is not always convenient. It actually may never be convenient for you. It is required, however, to maximize weight loss, to hold onto muscle, and to maintain that lost weight. What you pick for an activity is less important than the length of time you do it. Duration, or time spent, *burns more fat than intensity* of exercise.

Initially, your exercise must fit your health situation. Do you have lower back pain or bad knees? Are you short-winded when you rush around? Do you have the stamina to walk, jog, or run? Is a stationary bike or treadmill more to your liking? Would you be more likely to exercise in your home, outside in the neighborhood, or in an exercise facility? Would you prefer an exercise buddy or would you like to exercise by yourself? Answer these questions before spending time and money on exercise equipment or a gym membership. Exercise should be convenient to begin. If the gym is more than five minutes away, you may never get there. *The neighborhood never moves, and it begins at your back door.* Choose convenience over inconvenience, and immediate access over travel time to an exercise spot. *In our opinion, there is no comparison between a convenient daily neighborhood walk and a chance at once a week at the gym—take to the street.*

Physical activity helps you lose weight by increasing metabolism and burning calories. Metabolism can be defined as the number of calories burned. If you burn more calories than you store, you should lose weight. Physical activity helps reduce total body fat, especially abdominal fat. Fat in your midsection puts you at higher risk for heart disease and diabetes, as well as high cholesterol, high triglycerides, and high blood pressure. Having a combination of some of these

"You do not need to like your exercise, you just need to be willing to do it and not hate it."

abnormalities represents the metabolic syndrome. Those who have it are at higher risk of a shorter life span.

Exercise can decrease blood pressure, sugar, and insulin, and can promote an increase in HDL, the good cholesterol. Heart disease risk could decrease, and the heart becomes a more efficient pump. Osteoporosis can be prevented or delayed. Muscle mass could increase. Each pound of muscle burns 50 calories per day, while each pound of fat burns only 2 calories per day.

But you may ask yourself, how much exercise is enough? Is there a best exercise? Participating in moderate-to-intense physical activities results in significant health and fitness benefits. Activity can even be accumulated in small, multiple bouts at different times throughout the day and still burn enough calories over time to be functional for a weight loss plan and muscle mass preservation. Moderate-to-intense activity can be defined as brisk walking at a regular pace for 30 minutes or more. If it is too cold or wet outside, walk in a shopping mall. Work in the yard, or golf without a cart. Exercise with a buddy, join a class, or use an exercise video or DVD. Explore all options to help guarantee success.

Crosstraining provides a variety of activities to work different joints and muscles to decrease repeated joint and muscle stress. Using different muscles groups helps strengthen more of your body's muscle mass. Using different muscle groups decreases the risk of injury from overuse. Variety in activity also decreases the chance of boredom. Crosstraining includes activity such as walking, the stationary bike, weight machines, the treadmill, the elliptical machine, and the stair stepper. Swimming, hiking, outside bike riding and all the fun seasonal sports could be on your exercise acceptable list. If it keeps you moving, it is exercise.

How fast your heart rate should be for moderate exercise is based on first knowing your maximum heart rate (max HR). Max HR is a calculated number measured by the following formula: 220 minus your age in years. It is the heart rate that should not be reached during exercise. For moderate exercise, your heart rate should be 50% to 70% of max HR.

It is important to visit your doctor before beginning any exercise program to make sure it is safe for you.

Increasing the amount of time spent moving around during the workday should be part of your healthy weight plan. It is a less structured way to burn calories, but it does burn them. Physical activity plays a role that is supportive and rarely works as a single technique to drive your weight down. This is not a reason to avoid exercise. Successful weight loss is most predictable when exercise occurs regularly. Any type of exercise works if it is done with consistency.

Physical activity is the best predictor of weight success. Experience and knowledge bear this out. There is no perfect exercise. There is only that which suits your needs. Choose what you likely will want to do again and again. You do not need to like your exercise, you just need to be willing to do it and not hate it. So make your choice simple. Do what you can afford in both time and dollars. You probably will not use a lot of equipment. Unused exercise equipment becomes a clothes hanger and an object of scorn and guilt; it can be found at every yard sale. Maybe your first piece of equipment should come from a yard sale.

Once your choice has been made, you need a schedule for your exercise. Remember that being a weekend warrior may make you feel good about a hard workout on Saturday and Sunday, but it is not as healthy as a less intense working out five to seven days a week—slower, steady, frequent and maybe even less intense may be a formula for long-term success.

A 30-minute session is often recommended, but working up to that level and then pushing it to an hour is better. Intensity should be a gradual process. Your biggest enemy is a strained muscle, a bone bruise, a tendon tear, or a sore hip, knee, or back. Don't let pride drive you to overwork. Ending up with an injury can stop your plan and slow your progress. Monitoring exercise is important, since it is the most unnatural part of your weight management plan. Remember, a diary or journal is helpful.

The great advantage of physical activity is that it helps reduce total body fat, especially abdominal stomach fat. Risks of certain types of cancer also are decreased. Exercise strengthens heart muscle and allows oxygen-rich blood to be more efficiently carried to all muscles. With exercise resulting in a decrease in the risk of chronic diseases, it therefore increases the likelihood of a longer life span. It helps to relieve stress and possibly mild depression. Focusing on a goal is easier with less stress. With regular exercise,

sleep improves and energy
increases throughout the
day. Exercise may even delay
wrinkling by increasing the
oxygen supply to the skin.

"Food can be an addiction. Food
can be self-medication. Food can be
a friend. Food has the potential for
abuse."

There are two types of
physical activity: *aerobic and anaerobic*. Aerobic activity burns calories using oxygen as fuel. It is low intensity with nonlabored breathing, leading to longer exercise sessions. Anaerobic activity burns calories without oxygen. It is high intensity, requiring short durations of exercise.

While you may be able to thrive on exercise, it is food that can be considered a drug. Food can be an addiction. Food can be self-medication. Food can be a friend. Food has the potential for abuse. Structure, planning, and recognizing your successes will break down these barriers.

Remember that meal planning is the best way to get control of your eating habits. It helps you balance your nutritional intake. It helps you control cravings and become more satisfied with smaller portion sizes. Without a plan, how will you know whether you are eating enough of the foods to get the vitamins, minerals, and fiber needed to keep you healthy and allow you to lose weight consistently? A calendar on the refrigerator with your meals written on it makes day-to-day decision making less stressful.

Start tracking your eating times. What time do you eat breakfast, lunch, and dinner? Compare your eating times with these healthy suggestions: Eat breakfast within two hours of getting up to help get your metabolism started. Space each meal out to about every four to five hours throughout the day. Eating and not skipping meals may propel rather than slow down your ability to burn calories and better promote healthy weight. Eat meals at approximately the same times each day. Finish eating dinner at least four hours before bedtime. This allows digestion to be complete before going to sleep. Even if you choose to initially select food portions to be your focus, you must add food choice selection to be most effective.

Total calories needed for the day will vary based on age, sex, body size, and activity level. Learn from your doctor or health provider how to determine your resting metabolic rate (RMR). Your RMR is a calculated estimate of your daily, nonexercising calorie needs and what is necessary to maintain your current weight. To lose weight, you will need to consume less than this total number of calories in a day. Check with your doctor to confirm that eating less than this calorie count is safe and appropriate for you.

Your *emotions*—such as joy, sorrow, love, hate, or guilt—can affect how you eat. Some feelings are pleasant to experience while others are not so pleasant. As a response to these feelings, or emotions, you may overindulge in food or drink. Recognize these emotional states and you will be able to intercept your behavior. Emotions are sometimes linked to hunger. When you experience an emotion, you may simultaneously experience an urge to eat, but this is a false hunger. When you hear or feel your stomach growl, it does not mean that you need to eat. It is common to confuse emotional hunger with real hunger. As you identify your triggering emotions, this urge to eat will diminish. To help you deal with the tough times, try surrounding yourself with low-fat, low-calorie versions of the foods you typically choose. To keep portion sizes small, choose the smallest package or portion you can find.

You must learn to *problem solve.* Eating problems, some of which have been discussed earlier, include compulsive eating, anger eating, stress eating, comfort eating, binge eating, and nighttime eating, and they all stem from an inability to manage emotions. If you find yourself engaged in these self-defeating behaviors, pay better attention to your emotional side. Listen to what your body is telling you. Get reattached to your feelings. Recognize the differences between true hunger and an emotional urge to eat. *Take time to respond, not react.* Think about your eating choices. Choose a response other than eating. Wait 15 minutes before you consider food as the answer. Go for a walk, read a book, or call someone to chat.

> "Take time to respond, not react."

At mealtime, make eating a conscious effort. Eat more slowly. Take more time to allow the effects of your food to register in your brain. It takes about 20 minutes for the message, "I'm full" to get to your fullness center in your brain. Slow down your eating by taking smaller bites, putting down your utensils after each bite, and chewing every bite thoroughly. Remember: Stop eating on the run or on the road; you detract from feeling the sensation of fullness. Avoid feeling unsatisfied or wanting more. Don't eat and drive or eat when watching TV. Avoid eating and reading or eating and working at your desk. Don't stand and eat. Have a designated eating area.

2.4. As principal, you must ensure each student has a qualified teacher and provide a comprehensive professional growth plan for each faculty member that includes a personal healthy weight and wellness component so that he or she can serve as an appropriate role model to students.

One of the first actions you must take as the principal is to provide the necessary training or staff development for teachers to learn about their own health. Historically, staff development has been conducted at the district level. This process has continued to some degree, but usually these sessions at the district level are for motivational or introductory purposes. In most school systems today, much of the ongoing staff development is at the local school level conducted by experts in the field either within the school district or from an outside agency or consultant. Listed below is the model of a faculty wellness plan we have conducted with hundreds of teachers. Participants tell us that it is easy to follow because most faculty are involved, it increases faculty morale, and it improves the relationship between teachers and the principal. Finally, it opens the door to start working with children on wellness and the related topics of good nutrition and wellness.

School Wellness Organizational Design for Faculty and Staff Wellness

  I. *School Wellness Plan:* This wellness plan or program is designed for what level or group? Who are the individuals in the group?

 II. *Mission Statement for Wellness Program:* What is the intention, the purpose?

III. *Major Focus Areas:* What is the major goal or goals?

IV. *Specific Objectives:* What are the specific objectives?

 V. *Personal Plans* are embedded here.

VI. *Activities:* Include how each objective will be achieved—in detail.

VII. *Checkpoints:* Detail points in time to check progress; usually every two weeks minimally, but weekly checkpoints are ideal.

VIII. *Facilities, Equipment, Materials, Instructors/Trainers, and Medical Personnel:* This will vary greatly according to the type and degree of program that you want to develop and the budget and funding support available.

IX. *Budget and Funding Support:* What will the overall costs be for the program? Remember that start-up costs tend to be higher if you need equipment and specialized materials. Think sponsors, grants, and donations!!!

X. *Assessment of the Wellness Program:* How successful was the program? How will you determine the success? Assessment should be based on group and individual progress. Averages and ranges are useful here, if available.

XI. *Next Steps:* Will the wellness program continue? New directions? Modifications? Additional funding?

2.5. As the leader for the staff development of teachers in your school, you must provide training opportunities for faculty to learn concepts in health and wellness, in addition to instructional techniques for implementing integrated instruction within the classroom.

Schools have natural divisions that might be targeted for interventions. For example, we have integrated some suggestions given by the Department of Health and Human Services in their program announcement titled *School-Based Interventions to Prevent Obesity* (2004).

Focus could be centered on the content of the school curriculum where teachers would be able to use their established teaching skills. This would involve grade-level courses for teaching methodologies in specific disciplines such as mathematics, science, history, reading, social studies, earth science, health, and literature. Curriculum changes need to be designed to teach and encourage healthy food choices and active lifestyles. Behavior modification is a tool to attain healthy diets and active lifestyles. An end point is an increase in physical activity and a decrease in the amount of time devoted to sedentary activities, such as watching TV or playing computer games. Such interventions might be coupled with periods of increased physical activity before, during, or after school.

Interventions also should be designed to induce and maintain long-term behavioral changes in eating habits, food choices, exercise habits, and lifestyle.

Staff education should be inclusive of teachers, administrative staff, school nurses, food service personnel, school counselors, and student advisors. Changes may be necessary in school food service programs for school breakfast and school lunch. This is rapidly becoming reality as local, state and federal government officials have established task forces to address these issues. It is your time to be the initiator rather than the implementer of such programs.

Another point is that providing some education for parents who prepare their children's school lunch or provide the money for such lunches will better support the school's efforts and avoid undermining the school establishing new healthy habits for students and their teachers.

The Department of Health and Human Services recommends schools to improve physical activity programs and look to change the school environment. As the principal, you must look for synergy between interventions in curriculum changes and needed changes in the school environment.

Another major purpose of instituting these interventions is to gather baseline data from your school children in a controlled fashion to assess outcomes. Outcome assessment leads to better programs for your school year after year.

The Centers for Disease Control, in the recent publication *Guidelines for School Health Programs to Promote Lifelong Healthy Eating* (1996), stated that school-based programs can play an important role in promoting lifelong healthy eating and that "dietary factors contribute substantially to the burden of preventable illness and premature death in the USA." The national health promotion and disease prevention objectives encourage schools to provide nutrition education from preschool through 12th grade. This publication's recommendations, including interventions that promote healthy eating and physical activity behaviors during childhood and adolescence, may not only prevent some of the leading causes of illness and death but also decrease direct health care costs and improve the quality of life. Those are powerful incentives that empower a principal to encourage teachers to make a profound contribution to the well-being of their students.

The *Dietary Guidelines for Americans 2005* (Department of Health and Human Services, 2005) is designed to be the basis for school-based nutrition education. With this as a guide, all schools can play their role in meeting national health objectives. The CDC (1996) guidelines point out that *children and adolescents may be familiar with general relationships between nutrition and health but not details of the relationship between specific foods and health.* It may be obvious that high fat is not healthy and too much salt raises blood pressure, but students may not know what most foods contain.

Adolescents are better informed than younger children but lack the knowledge or motivation to act on what they know. From the CDC perspective, schools are ideal settings for nutrition (and physical activity) education for various reasons:

1. Schools can reach almost all school-age children.

2. Schools provide opportunities to practice healthy eating (and exercise) habits.

3. Schools can teach students how to resist social pressures.

4. Skilled school personnel are available and, after appropriate training, teachers can use their instructional skills, and food service personnel can contribute their expertise (and administrators can encourage and support) to nutrition (and exercise) education programs.

5. Studies support that school-based initiatives can improve the behaviors of our students (p. 11).

The CDC guidelines recommend a coordinated school nutrition policy be adopted that promotes healthy eating through classroom lessons and a supportive "school environment." A school environment is supportive when nutrition (and exercise) education is reinforced throughout the experience of the school day. When nutrition education is occurring in the classroom, it should be complemented by the breakfast and lunch options served in the cafeteria plus what is available in the snack and drink machines,

If drink machines are available, they will soon be removed from most elementary and middle schools. Awareness of classroom snacks and celebrations, using food as a reward or disallowing food as a punishment, needs to be addressed. What foods are sold at school-sponsored events, including sports and fund-raising, should be a focus of change. The CDC report and we as authors emphasize that *establishing a new school environment policy without a unified coordinated nutrition and exercise attitude can have a negative, rather than a positive, influence on student commitment, acceptance, and action.* To establish a policy, input may be needed from widely diverse school and possibly outside sources. A school health committee or a nutrition advisory committee may be effective in galvanizing a school plan and fostering needed changes in the school environment. Committee members should be chosen for skills brought to the table and commitment to the task at hand. These are the most important attributes when choosing committee members. Consider including the following as members:

a. Students

b. Class teachers and physical education teachers

c. Coaches

d. Administrative staff

e. Food service personnel

f. School nurses if available

g. School counselors

h. Parents

i. Ethnic representation

Remember to address local concerns, food preferences, and varied dietary and ethnic practices in the community. Committee members from outside the school system should be considered because of the experience and manpower they can bring to your mission. If their membership is not possible, then these special interest groups could be asked to attend a focused meeting or to provide information. These are outside organizations to consider:

1. American Dietetic Association
2. American Heart Association
3. American Cancer Society
4. University faculty
5. Nutrition unit within the State Department of Health
6. District or state school health coordinator
7. Local Women, Infants and Children (WIC) program director
8. Cooperative extension nutrition education program
9. American School Food Service Association
10. School food and beverage provider
11. Local restaurant or fast food establishment
12. Grocery store manager
13. Medical professionals
14. Public Health Department

Remember that active behavior learning occurs best when it is fun, it is participatory, and it emphasizes positive aspects of health and wellness. Presentation of new information needs to be in the context of what is important to the student, and this definitely varies, as you well know, by age group. The CDC guidelines pose a proactive role for the school cafeteria director, suggesting visits to classrooms, invitations to students to see cooks in action, and even student involvement in planning menus and providing recipes. Feedback from students, teachers, and parents may help to fine-tune the program. Reinforce learning by repetition in the class-room, posters in the cafeteria as reminders of nutrition facts, and helpful hints for parents imbedded in monthly cafeteria menus that can be sent to the student's home. Presentation at parent association meetings and question-and-answer sessions may help solidify support for your program to make decisions on activity requirements in your school. We have included activity terminology that has been constant for several decades.

Definitions:

Exercise is a subset of physical activity. It is planned, structured, and repetitive and done to improve or maintain physical fitness.

Health-related fitness includes heart and lung endurance, muscular strength and endurance, flexibility, and body definition.

Physical activity is any bodily motion produced by skeletal muscles that results in energy expenditure.

Physical education is skill and coordination focused.

Physical fitness is a subset of exercises that are either health or skill related.

Skill-related fitness includes balance, agility, power, reaction time, speed, and coordination.

Unstructured physical activity includes walking, bicycling, and playing activity (Caspersen, Powell, & Christenson, 1985).

Listed below are school activity goals:

1. Physical education must be provided daily to all elementary school students and middle school students K–8.

2. Daily recess periods are needed for elementary school students coupled with supervised unstructured play.

3. Physical activity should be embedded in the core curriculum and available to all children, including those with special medical needs.

4. Physical activity should be included in afterschool programs.

5. School facilities should be made available to students, families, and the community for physical activity after school hours and on weekends. Supervision could be shared with the community.

6. Walking to school with parent supervision should be promoted, and bike racks should be provided.

Since schools are a major site of food intake and activity, there will be very little variation needed in the instruction, advice, and support given to weight-healthy individuals and to those at an unhealthy weight. All students will improve their health with a better-organized focus on nutrition and exercise. Teachers have the skills to teach what they understand. *Emphasis in teacher training needs to be on content and teaching strategies. Focus should be on teachers learning interactive instructional skills and not on lectures.* We believe in and recommend never lecturing to students more than 15 minutes during any 50- to 90-minute period.

Visual aids have always been a time-honored teaching tool. Principals, teachers, school nurses, and cafeteria managers should be thinking about how to portray in graphic fashion positive, attractive nutrition messages in the cafeteria and exercise messages in classrooms and the gymnasium. Images and words can have strong meaning if consistent with the target age group and when reinforced by teacher action.

Teaching content is critical for establishing improved long-time habits. There are no proven school system road maps in the country that have significant outcome data to tell you the best way to teach and demonstrate what is needed. Many approaches to promote a healthier weight in our youth have been attempted. The focus has usually been on a single goal, such as preventing soda machine usage during school hours or mandating broad changes in the cafeteria and with physical education. Unfortunately, change recommendations, big or small, have historically not been generated by the educators of our children and adolescents. *You have had too little input into the process under which you may have to govern.*

2.6. With direct input from powerful special interest groups, professional organizations, and the food and beverage industry, you must be proactive in implementing successful programs for overweight and obese students. As the school principal, you must develop partnerships with civic organizations, local businesses, medical professionals, and the media to obtain the necessary human and financial resources needed to support the implementation of the above program.

School partnerships should be explored between students, the business community, the medical community, the media, city/county government, the parks and recreation department, the local health department, the board of education, and local exercise facilities such as the YMCA and other commercial exercise establishments. Also include walking, running, and biking organizations. Local dieticians, chiropractors, and independent experts should also play a significant role. *The goal is not to reinvent the wheel but to channel expertise possibly already in existence, focusing them on common goals without competing with their business objectives.* By identifying community activities already engaged in combating childhood and adolescent unhealthy weight, you must partner with them toward a common goal rather than be competitive with these organizations.

A variety of news reports have reported on states that have been aggressive in the prevention of childhood and adolescent obesity. To list a few: Arkansas, North Carolina, Kentucky, and California. Other important state initiatives include Texas reinstating a rule requiring elementary school children to take a minimum of 135 minutes of physical education every week. This reversed a 1995 law that characterized physical education as an elective course. A progressive program in California known as Children's Five a Day Power Play uses a multichannel community-based approach to encourage children ages 9–11 and their families to be physically active and eat at least five servings of fruits/vegetables every day as part of a low-fat, high-fiber diet. The Power Play campaign involves regional organizations to oversee partnering and implementation of the Power Plan campaign in schools, community youth organizations, farmers' markets, supermarkets, food services/restaurants, and through local media exposure.

Connecticut requires physical activity daily from kindergarten through fifth grade. If a child does not have a gym class on any one day, the school must offer recess. The law also requires schools to sell low-fat dairy products, water, and fruit.

North Carolina Health and Wellness Trust Fund Commission was charged by the North Carolina General Assembly to address the health needs of vulnerable and underserved populations and to develop comprehensive, community-based plans with goals and objectives to improve health and wellness. Grant funds to implement pilot programs addressing childhood obesity in communities across the state are in full progress. A subcommittee for Childhood Overweight and Obesity, called Fit Families NC, has a core goal of creating policy changes related to nutrition and physical activity. Several legislative proposals have been passed by the 2005 state legislature, including mandating 30 minutes of physical activity daily in all elementary schools. This activity is in addition to physical education and recess times. School drink machines will be off limits until after lunch, and no more than half of the drinks for sale can contain sugar. Water will be available in all drink machines, and no soft drink machines will be in elementary schools.

North Carolina's "Eat Smart Move More . . . North Carolina" is a statewide initiative that promotes increased opportunities for healthy eating and physical activity. Their recommended standards for all foods available in schools have been published.

Massachusetts has one of the largest Safe Routes to Schools programs encouraging children to walk or bike to school with parent escorts. The state offered pedestrian-safety training and advocates for easier-to-navigate sidewalks, crosswalks, and streets.

A greater discussion of what some other states and school systems are doing is provided in Chapter 3.

2.7. The school principal provides a safe and orderly environment to confront and resolve negative issues impacting the overall growth and academic achievement of all students, including those who are overweight and obese.

A Case History of Insensitivity and Poor Understanding

A classroom teacher wanted to promote increased physical activity and integrate it with teaching her students. To that end, she had her students walk slowly once, and sometimes more, around the school track daily during their class time. Upon returning to the classroom, they went to the map in the classroom and plotted 100 miles for each trip around the track. The trip started at the school site and moved west across the country. The goal was to learn about the major cities they passed through in this virtual tour of the United States. To accomplish this, the class wrote letters to Chambers of Commerce of approaching cities asking for information about their communities. That information became the basis for geography, history, economic, and social studies topics. The plan was abruptly stopped when a parent complained to the school principal. She objected to her daughter being forced to walk on the school track because she was too tired when she got home. This mother told the principal that if "that fat teacher wanted to exercise, let her do it on her own time." At a meeting called by the principal, the teacher was told to stop her virtual tour of the United States.

The teacher should have had the opportunity to talk with the principal in private. An alternative lesson plan could have been developed for the student in question, which would have allowed the other students to continue with their original project.

As a responsible principal, it is imperative that you use your knowledge and ability to collaborate with diverse students (including overweight and obese students) and family members to promote student success by acting with fairness, with integrity, and in an ethical manner.

Outreach to the community has support value to you as principal and to your school, as well as encouraging the feel-good atmosphere developed when communities help their young people. Civic organization and large businesses usually have causes that they support. This support is usually provided on a yearly basis or longer. A civic organization's or business's decision to take up a cause is usually made at a fixed time—usually at the beginning of the fiscal year. You, the principal, need a school committee to develop a needs plan for presentation to civic and business organizations. These organizations could supply

- funds in the form of gifts, grants, or awards;
- trained people to help with developing strategies, execution of existing programs, and short- and long-range planning;
- manpower to provide people for specific tasks; and
- open doors to other options including local and state government.

Local and state governments may be another source of help to you and your school. The mayor, city council, and local board of education may be accepting of a sound school program to implement.

Enlightened members of the medical community would look at a request to provide some type of instruction and support in the school as an extension of their educational responsibilities to children. This support should be sought from pediatricians and their staff—either personally or through the local pediatric society; and hospital administrators, who could supply dieticians, nurses, and patient educators to assist in your school needs plan. Hospitals could also provide a location for meetings of staff, students, parents, and PTO members, as well as an advertising source.

CHAPTER THREE

The Barriers We Face

All of the great leaders have had one characteristic in common: it was the willingness to confront unequivocally the major anxiety of their people in their time. This, and not much else, is the essence of leadership.

—John Kenneth Galbraith

Critical Question 3

How can the principal as instructional leader of the school remove internal and external barriers that negatively impact success?

THE ESSENTIAL TRUTHS

3.1. Principals must become positive role models.

3.2. Parental resistance to solving weight problems can be transferred to children.

3.3. Students can create self-barriers.

3.4. Weight discrimination can be a barrier created by your teachers and reinforced by other students.

3.5. Structural barriers within the school system promote unhealthy food and beverage choices.

3.6. Stress and overeating are barriers to controlling the obesity epidemic.

3.7. Transitions and resistance to change are barriers.

PRACTICAL GUIDES TO THE ESSENTIAL TRUTHS

3.1. Principals must become positive role models.

Over 60% of school superintendents, teachers, and parents are overweight or obese. Historically, adults have not served as positive role models for healthy weight for children. Children learn from us and they model our behaviors. That is one of the major ways we transfer the culture to the next generation in a process we refer to as informal education.

We transfer culture formally through the instructional process, but as educators we know that modeling is one of the most effective forms of teaching. Unfortunately, it does not matter if our modeling is intentional or unintentional. Children learn from us whether we model a healthy weight *or* an unhealthy weight. Your teachers get their motivation from you, getting their cues from your emphasis and prerogatives. A principal must be willing to be an example and the generator of change. Since American adults are chronically overweight and getting bigger by the year, modifying weight, exercise, and associated behaviors can be a significant barrier to any well-meaning principal. No one intentionally sets himself or herself up to fail, but failure is less likely when the goal is an admirable one. Trying is starting on the road to succeed. Principals are always in the spotlight, and making a personal change is for the betterment of yourself, your teachers, and the students.

3.2. Parental resistance to solving weight problems can be transferred to children.

A fatalistic or uncaring attitude about obesity or wellness by parents, a major lack of personal success in dealing with their own long-term weight problems, or an inability to deal with sustained change can easily be transferred to children.

Parental perception of a child's weight as a problem varies considerably. If a parent recognizes a child's weight as a family trait, it may be considered not only insurmountable but also unworthy of efforts to overcome it. Parental experience may have been one of failure coupled with an unwillingness to expose their child to, or possibly even to set their child up for, failure. What is learned in school may be negated by family habits practiced at home.

Lack of parental involvement and lack of understanding of the medical, social, and psychological consequences of unhealthy weight is prevalent in the population. Most Americans are only now becoming concerned with their own weight and the weight of their children. It remains a hard sell, however, to convince adults to change, and that fact places their children at risk. Even though the majority of American adults are now overweight, one out of four adults still does not believe that his or her weight or the weight of his or her overweight children is a serious problem. You can't help fix a problem if it is not perceived as one.

Parental and personal expectations of weight loss success can have a significant impact on weight loss goals for children. How well adolescents will focus on change may be influenced by positive parental involvement. Parents are the behavior change motivators within the family. Youngsters feel more secure in making changes in their eating habits when parents make it a family affair. Children actually do learn better by observing what their role models do rather than by listening to what they say. A majority of parents, when given the tools, will be more motivated and better equipped to reinforce the health positives their children have learned and brought home from school. Providing parents with information about the goals for preventing and addressing unhealthy weight in your school may be a highly significant family health event.

Delivering information and action plans to parents so as to not offend or anger also may be a barrier. To engage parents in the process takes an understanding of parental awareness and personal sensitivities. Parental beliefs about their personal role in the unhealthy weight of their children vary in accordance with their own self-confidence and self-assuredness as well as what they perceive as their

> An educated student may be a teacher to the family and an agent of family change.

role in the health of the family. All family members, some with different levels of tolerance for change, have the potential to enhance, encourage, or sabotage weight-management goals. A tactful teacher or principal may intervene to depersonalize the situation and gain greater parental support, but in time the parent must accept responsibility to be an agent of change in order to maximize success. In one local school system where we are working with several school principals and teachers, assisting them in integrating nutrition and physical activity into the school day, a mother spoke with her child's teacher about her young daughter reading the ketchup bottle label one evening at the dinner table. Her child commented on the amount of sugar ketchup contained. The mother wanted to know how her daughter knew this fact and why it was important. It could have been a confrontational situation, but the teacher explained the goals of the school program, and the mother walked away as an advocate of change for her family. This was not a major event in the life of this family, but it did create a sense of awareness of calories. A conversation about healthy family eating was begun in this household.

Please keep in mind that if an overweight child is a member of a significantly overweight family, you as an educator will have minimal influence over this genetic trait. However, the potential exists to prevent further weight gain, and this can be a major positive outcome of education. There is a large environmental component that influences body weight, and this may be affected in a positive way by nutrition education, behavior change, and exercise, when provided by the school experience.

> The prevention of weight gain rather than weight loss is also a victory for the principal when it comes to the health of your teachers and students. The end point of classroom education and role modeling will affect students in different ways and to different degrees. Prevention has a longer effect on children who are at risk for becoming an unhealthy weight—possibily a lifelong preventative effect. It is fair to say, therefore, that since we have a public health crisis in childhood overweight, all students benefit, regardless of their current body weight or their activity level.

3.3. Students can create self-barriers.

Students themselves may constitute a major barrier to addressing the obesity epidemic, especially if limited knowledge of nutrition, unhealthy eating habits, and/or lack of proper exercise is magnified by other direct or indirect factors. Students will not be interested or engaged unless they see the value in it for them. Student prejudice against overweight peers can be major, vicious, and discriminatory. It can surface in such an environment. Time needed to defuse discrimination may be more frustrating than effective. The overweight student may be reluctant to be active and chance being the center of possible criticism. The passive student may not wish to get involved at all. This can be a barrier to teachers who wish to follow your lead but see time as an insurmountable barrier. Constructive time must be spent on teacher education, continuing education, and lesson planning to prepare them for the task.

> Principals cannot be effective in changing the school's role in the childhood obesity epidemic unless they focus on the student as a major barrier. Limited knowledge of nutrition, unhealthy eating habits, and/or lack of proper exercise are prevalent and magnified by other direct or indirect factors.

To minimize this barrier, emphasis must be on creating an academic environment where all students can excel. Your plan should include a school committee to help design and implement the plan. We provided a suggested list of committee members in Chapter 2.

3.4. Weight discrimination can be a barrier created by your teachers and reinforced by other students.

Negative behaviors and emotions felt by overweight students may be magnified by stigmatizing words or actions on the part of other youth and even some adults, including principals, teachers, and other school personnel. Educators may not be verbally suspect, but actions, lack of actions, or body language can be a barrier. Such prejudice may be a result of discrimination or the

Weight discrimination, stigma, and prejudices are barriers created or perpetuated by teachers, fellow students, health professionals, and society in general.

misconception that unhealthy weight is synonymous with lack of personal control or lack of concern about one's appearance.

No teacher should participate in such belief systems or behavior. It will take constant diligence of the principal to create a nonprejudicial atmosphere in the school environment. This includes monitoring of staff members such as cafeteria personnel, counselors, school nurses, maintenance crew, volunteers, and so forth.

Case History of Obesity Discrimination

An eight-year-old boy, BW, was being made fun of in class by other boys because of his earlier poor performance in PE class. It all began with the PE teacher commenting on his weight and inferring that he should stay away from snack foods. The kids laughed and the PE teacher did nothing to stop them, and the badgering continued on into the next class. The class teacher silenced the noise, but did not criticize their negative comments about BW. Class order was restored by the teacher only because classwork was being disrupted. As a result of the teacher's actions, BW felt abandoned by his teacher and for the rest of the year did not feel comfortable in her class. BW had told his mother that he disliked his teacher, and when questioned, BW stated, "She was mean to me."

During the next parent-teacher conference, BW's mother inquired of the teacher about BW's statement about disliking her. The teacher was shocked! Both she and the PE teacher had no idea or recall of their inappropriate supportive roles in discriminating against BW.

The training that you provide for your teachers should create a greater awareness of this type of sensitive situation.

In seminars with teachers today, we often ask the audience if anyone knew a fellow student who had been humiliated or called names because of being overweight. Every hand is always raised. Weight discrimination is still occurring every day in schools today.

3.5. Structural barriers within the school system promote unhealthy food and beverage choices.

Structural barriers to weight control and weight loss have been built into the school and educational system. These include

- limitation or removal of health and physical education from the curriculum;
- allowing competitive foods to dominate the cafeteria menu (competitive foods offered at lunchtime do help pay the food service bills, and the economics of this needs to be addressed before real changes can be made in the cafeteria);
- allowing fund-raising activities that focus on *selling* unhealthy foods; and
- selling unhealthy foods and beverages at school sporting events or any school-sanctioned event.

Allowing and promoting unhealthy foods and beverages through these school-related activities reinforce the messages you are trying to counter.

Beverage and Vending Contracts

School systems across the country negotiate exclusive pouring and vending contracts, either with single or with multiple major providers of beverage and snack machines. Dynamic changes are happening in this arena, especially in vending machine contracts, where new agreements between schools and the industry will significantly limit the sale of sugar containing drinks. What will happen to the commissions schools make from beverage contracts, including industry dollars for school sports scoreboards and other signage, ice machines and financial support of promotional events, educational supplies, and student awards, which were other by-products of these contracts, is in question. School systems that sign these contracts have a responsibility to the students and faculty who eat and drink from these machines and purchase them at school events. These beverages and snacks are being consumed with increasing frequency and can have health and weight consequences.

What must become the norm is not only the emphasis on 100% fruit juice, low-fat milk, and water as the major components in drink machines, but also alternative foods continuing to be made available at school events and in the school cafeteria. Healthy changes related to food and drink purchased at school should keep the overall health message to students on target and further aid in controlling the epidemic of overweight children.

Our Recommendation

Until a given school district makes innovative healthy eating decisions, there are creative changes that principals can make with the help of the school cafeteria director and the appointed school dietitian. Take the sale of pizza, for example: the choices could be limited to a cheese or a veggie pizza. Another change might be limiting drink sales to only water, 100% fruit juice, and diet sodas at school events.

A La Carte Foods in School Cafeterias

A la carte food sales in a school's cafeteria represent about one-third of the cafeteria's revenue. Most cafeterias could not be self-supporting without the sale of these foods to supplement the money they receive from federal reimbursement from sales of USDA breakfasts and lunches. All principals know that the revenue from federal meal reimbursement is about one-third of the cost to schools for the total preparation and providing of these meals to students and faculty.

A la carte foods—also known as *competitive foods*—tend to be foods with higher fat, higher calorie, and/or higher sugar content as well as lower nutritional value as compared to the USDA National School Lunch Program and School Breakfast Program standards (USDA, 2001). Competitive foods tend to mimic the food choices made by students when eating meals outside of the school day. National standards for dietary guidelines should determine what is served in schools, but as long as schools have the financial burden of making up revenue shortfalls, a la carte foods are likely to remain available for sale in school cafeterias. Unfortunately, it is been our observation that these foods are the most desirable and often the first choice of many students. Where else, for example, could a student get a slice of pizza and French fries for lunch?

Role Models

As noted in sections 3.1 and 3.2, children take life cues as much from what they observe as from what they are taught. If a teacher or school administrator at an unhealthy weight is perceived by staff and students as making a personal effort to improve, then that adult is sending a powerful message of self-efficacy and self-betterment to multitudes of students. But with 61% of the adult population at an unhealthy weight, teachers and school administrators also are at high risk of modeling behaviors that are barriers to their students making progress toward healthy weight.

There are crosscurrents in every school that can undermine students making commitments to healthy life changes, including:

- wanting to eat healthier foods but having the stimulus of unhealthy food and drink choices that are too readily available when students are hungry, and no stimulus to curtail making poor choices;
- needing structured school exercises—students exist and participate in an environment where they have too many sedentary activities; and
- needing health education, physical education, nutrition education, and wellness education as part of the PreK–12 core curriculum but having those subjects short-changed or removed from the curriculum entirely.

Until these structural barriers within the school system can be removed, our children and the adults who teach them will inevitably find that the stimulus to change will be short lived and temporary at best. The health and education advancement of all students will remain in jeopardy.

3.6. Stress and overeating are barriers to controlling the obesity epidemic.

Adults were never taught time and stress management in any formal setting while in school. We did not learn how to manage priorities or to change priorities when they were out of control and affecting our stress levels. Nothing has changed, except our knowledge that uncontrolled stress is a major cause of overeating. When stress is prolonged or unresolved, it interferes with our ability to function both physically and emotionally. School children are not immune to this stress response.

Educational leaders of the 21st century face many challenges, including change at various levels, conflict, and internal and external pressures. For principals, stress may result from routine administrative duties, which include the following:

- A 60- to 80-hour work week
- A very heavy workload
- Supervision of afterschool activities
- Little pay difference between veteran teachers and administrators
- High expectations
- Mandates and paperwork
- Complex social problems

Stress also affects the principal's noninstructional responsibilities, which often include dealing with discipline problems and being on guard for gangs and extreme school violence, while excessive paperwork, memos for required meetings, and copies of the latest federal, state, and local mandates pile up on your desk (Queen & Queen, 2005). Implementing those constantly changing mandates can lead to still more stress as the principal encounters resistance to district policies from teachers and staff members who are concerned that a particular policy may not fit their needs and/or the needs of their students and community. Remember, stress is a major part of life. Everyone experiences various levels of stress, but what matters is how we handle it.

Elementary, middle, and high school principals experience similar types of stress, but excessive stress is not universal to all administrators. Excessive stress can lead not only to health problems, but also to burnout. Signs of burnout may include emotional exhaustion, which occurs when principals are emotionally drained on a psychological level from working at school; depersonalization, which may cause the principal to stop caring about people or events at school; and depression, which may lead to the principal turning the negative feelings inward and to a drop-off in personal accomplishment and energy both for personal and professional life.

Emotions and Stress

The emotions associated with stress include anxiety, guilt, anger, fear, resentment, and feelings of being overwhelmed and unloved. The medical problems associated with stress are a major reason for visits to the doctor, with patients reporting such symptoms as headache, fatigue, sleep disorders, stomach pain, and bowel problems. More serious medical problems associated with stress can even include heart disease and high blood pressure. Stress is also known to alter the body's hormonal balance, and it may impair the body's immune system, thereby decreasing the ability to fight off viruses and bacterial infections.

Prolonged stress can result in adverse behaviors. It can lead to poorer concentration, poorer decision making, poorer communication and organizational skills, poorer academic performance, and even absenteeism. Any change or life transition can bring on stress, and there are good stressors and bad stressors, and people vary in what triggers their stress responses. Internal stressors most often are personal thoughts and feelings. External stressors can include personal conflicts, demanding schedules and situations, physical challenges and illnesses, sudden or traumatic events, and so forth. Overeating, unfortunately, is a very common reaction to stress, especially when the stress involves anxiety and anger.

Overeating in Response to Anxiety, Anger, and Stress

Anxiety results in feelings of apprehension or worry about what might happen, keeping one at a disadvantage until the anxiety can be resolved. During periods of anxiety, many people react by overeating. Anxiety often occurs when people are facing something unfamiliar or something they prefer to avoid, but it also can occur for no apparent reason. People who learn to monitor their thoughts, feelings, and behaviors can learn to identify the person or event that triggered their anxiety and address the trigger directly. Overeating and poor food choices often are attempts to cover up anxious, angry, or otherwise uncomfortable emotions. As adults, we need to learn to manage our own stress responses. As educators, we can teach children the same lessons.

Anger also is a legitimate feeling. It is a reaction to something offensive that has occurred. Children are entitled to feel angry, too, and their anger is neither good nor bad. Anger can be used in

Stress is not limited to overweight children but the response to that stress may be different. All children can overeat, but not all will become overweight.

positive or negative ways. Reactions to anger may be helpful or harmful, especially when they result in overeating and poor food choices. We need to choose constructive responses.

3.7. Transitions and resistance to change are barriers.

Principals must learn to recognize which teachers are ready to make changes, and which are ready to learn. Several formal school transitions have been identified by Akos, Queen, and Lineberry (2005). All of these transitions or changes cause a degree of anxiety, but with strong cooperation among feeder schools, parents, faculty, and staff, programs can be developed to alleviate much of the pain of this process. Similar things can be done to reduce anxiety during a transition to wellness.

Readiness to Change

To make a change in eating, activity, or any established habit, for that matter, principals must be ready and committed to make the change. Assessing someone's readiness can be done through a readiness scale that identifies five levels of readiness for change. There are several variations of this scale available. Neither you, the principal, nor all of your teachers, their students, parents, or siblings will be at the same level of readiness for change. You must be a facilitator for your teachers in bringing them all to parity as quickly as possible. This will make change happen in your school with the least amount of resistance, frustration, and disruption. Starting change at the best stage of readiness helps prevent failure and increases the possibility for success.

Planning for Change

To recognize a person's level of readiness for change, examine the stages that people go through:

• *Stage 1—Precontemplation:* This stage occurs when someone does not yet appreciate that change is necessary. The plan at this level should be for awareness education. Awareness is paramount here, and lack of awareness is a barrier to be overcome.

- *Stage 2—Contemplation:* This is where you or one of your teachers appreciates that change does makes sense but is not yet ready to do something about it. If it is you, then change will not yet get off the ground. If it is one of your teachers, then it may be a delicate time for you since an unready teacher could be a saboteur in your midst. The plan for someone at this stage is more detailed education about what will happen.

- *Stage 3—Preparation:* When your teachers have a comfortable understanding of the problem and are getting ready to act, the stage is set to develop action plans compatible with needs and abilities.

- *Stage 4—Action:* When the first steps are taken, the planning focus is on further advancement in what was started. Keeping the momentum going can be a significant barrier to your school goal of healthy weight at this stage.

- *Stage 5—Results:* Hopefully the results are positive. The plan is to maintain the goals.

Conflicting Problems

I. While counseling a mother about her overweight 8- and 10-year-old sons, the nutrition and exercise plan discussed made sense to the mother and was accepted by the boys. Implementation, however, became a problem. Nightly, their father sabotaged the efforts made by mom and the boys. "Eat like me" was the father's portrayed message. The father promised to do fun exercises with the boys, but it never seemed to happen. Initial failure was due to parents not being at the same stage of readiness to change. Eventually both parents became close enough to Stage 4 readiness for the action plan to begin to take effect.

II. A teacher who shared the responsibility for writing lesson plans for the week for her grade level did not do her work; she was not yet committed. As a result, the teachers and their students lost instructional continuity in the classroom. Also missing that week was the feedback interaction between teachers about the effectiveness of the lesson plans.

If principals will target parents as participants in a school plan, the yield may be far-reaching with long-term benefit. The barriers here are significant since it is hard to get parental involvement. The better the message carried home to responsive parents and other household members, the better the healthy weight outcome and the greater the educational experience. Frequency of home communication may also play a role.

SCHOOLS ARE NEGATIVE EXERCISE ZONES

The school environment is currently a negative exercise zone. This unfortunate situation is not reinforcing to teachers or students who want to exercise, and it provides no stimulus to students who need encouragement to exercise. This is a barrier to successfully achieving or maintaining a healthy weight. One obvious problem is the de-emphasis of physical education and free-time school activities, especially in the younger grades. It is in the elementary school setting that the greatest impact will be felt. Principals must look toward innovative teachers and support their efforts to implement the curriculum.

In the community, there are fixed environmental issues that are beyond the control of the school. Unsafe areas for walking and lack of other community-based fitness opportunities for students and their families add to the problem.

SCHOOL BOARD, BOARD OF EDUCATION, AND PARENT ORGANIZATIONS AS BARRIERS

Since the level of understanding, interest, and political flavor of each of these groups may greatly vary, they may provide support or be a barrier. Involving community, business, and local government in your school plan may become a significant additive support or a barrier. Restraints of community organizations, business personal goals, and rules of government should play a role in attempting to establish any relationship. The process of defining what groups to contact and the interview process itself can be a barrier. Even though outside organizations may have their own agenda, you must decide to embrace their support if their goals do not conflict with yours and are not otherwise contrary to school policies.

HEALTH CARE PROVIDER KNOWLEDGE BASE AND INVOLVEMENT AS A BARRIER

The most visible and useful medical person in a school setting will be the school nurse. There may be one readily available to you or you may share a nurse with many other schools. Limited access to a school nurse is a barrier. Be aware that even those health care professionals and advocates of the health of your students are not immune to prejudice and weight discrimination against overweight children or adults.

Most children receive their health care in a pediatric or family practice setting, and barriers to healthy weight exist there, too. Contributing factors include such problems as time restraints on doctors, nurses, and nurse practitioners, as well as the need for more comprehensive education for doctors and their staffs in weight management approaches and techniques.

Until recently, pediatricians were inclined not to mention a child's unhealthy weight to parents, waiting instead for parents to voice their own concerns about the weight of their children. The American Pediatric Society is now encouraging pediatricians to play a more active role in the defining and addressing of unhealthy weight issues with the parents of unhealthy weight children and adolescents. Depending on your community, you may or may not be able to count on the medical community to be an active partner or resource. Even when called upon, pediatric doctors still do not have answers about childhood obesity. Medical expertise in this area is still an unmet community need. Answers are only now being studied and slowly put into medical practice. Health insurance reimbursement for medical care of weight management programs is insufficient to meet the growing and significant need and creates a barrier to medical attention and a barrier to support needed by schools that are doing their best to intervene in the childhood obesity epidemic.

CHAPTER FOUR

School Principal Action Plans

Critical Question 4

It appears that, as in many things in education, preventing and limiting childhood obesity and improving overall faculty and staff wellness should be a team approach, correct?

THE ESSENTIAL TRUTHS

4.1. The principal's plan for faculty health promotion should be a team approach.

4.2. The principal's plan for students' improved healthy weight and exercise should be a team approach.

4.3. Unhealthy weight impacts the emotional-social development of students. To address it, you need to better understand it.

PRACTICAL GUIDES TO
THE ESSENTIAL TRUTHS

4.1. The principal's plan for faculty
health promotion should be a team approach.

We have discussed the importance of the health of your teachers and other school staff members in Chapter 1. In this section, we outline a team faculty approach necessary to make a healthy action plan functional for your school. This includes a plan for students within the instructional environment and important information you need to know about the social and emotional impact obesity has on children. Not all school demographics are the same, and there will be special needs and some road blocks to success in all schools. Combining a team of school staff with some focused outside expertise may give you more insight in establishing goals for your school employees in addition to addressing any special needs and potential roadblocks to implementing your health promotion plan. A well-designed plan that is enthusiastically marketed by you and the team will go a long way toward encouraging even the most reluctant teacher or other staff member to be an active participant. Group education in nutrition and exercise is a positive way to create unity of purpose as well as to allow for individual success.

Teachers and other school personnel need the structure that a well-designed school-based plan provides. This can increase the odds for them to become successful in improving their own health. The knowledge gained will be self-serving and will create the improved self-worth and self-confidence that are consistent with healthy lifestyle changes. The better your teachers feel, the more productive they can be at teaching. Changes made while participating in the faculty health promotion will provide teachers with practical information as a template for the challenge of educating and instructing their students as well as the confidence needed to share some of this information with their students. In Chapter 1, we discussed the importance of teacher and faculty health. To develop such a program, a principal will need a planning and implementation team. Following is an example of the composition of such a team:

Principal's Team for Faculty and Staff Health Promotion

Mission: To establish reasonable healthy weight options and instructions for all academic staff members. Such a plan needs to be comprehensive and part of a continuing education plan.

Goals: (1) To improve school faculty and staff members' health. (2) To improve the ability of teachers and other personnel to teach, mentor, and support students. (3) To be role models for students.

Team Member Selection: Choose wisely when picking your team. This is neither a political appointment nor a popularity issue. You want thinkers, leaders, doers, and workers! The team must determine what is needed to reach the goal of improved school health for the staff and seek answers to such questions as these: Will your program include an initial medical screening? Will it include a written survey of health-related questions that help define an individual's health needs? Will there be laboratory tests to focus on defining common disease states? From a different perspective, team members may want to investigate what format or design would be the best for the wellness program; logistics such as who will be the coordinator and trainer; and perhaps even funding issues.

1. From the start, it will be important to select a teacher who will serve as the program liaison to the faculty and staff. This teacher will have the responsibility for providing much of the leadership in the successful implementation of the team plan. We suggest that a teacher from each grade level should be recruited to be the grade representative. This liaison need not initially be a planning team member and could be chosen by the team.

2. A physician or other medical professional is needed for advice on program content; this role is an important one. Several medical health assessment tools are available, and one will be needed for your faculty health promotion plan. Help may also be obtained from another planning team member, a local hospital representative. Either the medical professional or hospital team member could be a source for continuing education and lab screening capabilities for the plan. A trained paramedic, or perhaps the school nurse, if available, can assess weight, BMI, and blood pressure.

3. Choose one of the administrative team leaders as a representative from the principal's staff—ideally one with decision-making capabilities such as an assistant principal.

4. You will need a school nurse, if a nurse is available. His or her role could be to serve as the in-house coordinator of the program if he or she can be on your campus often enough to be effective. This individual may be able to play dual roles: in this position as well as that described in number 2.

5. A local hospital administrator could supply dieticians, nurses, exercise specialists, and laboratory staff to serve as implementers of those aspects of the plan, and perhaps could supply an advertising source. An exercise plans as part of the program may be advanced with the help of a local exercise facility if the hospital cannot serve this important role. The YMCA has been active nationally in health promotion and has cosponsored such programs. Other exercise facilities or organizations may be willing to assist. Hospitals could also provide a location for educational training meetings of staff, students, parents, and PTO members (however, the more meetings you can keep on your campus, the better control you have and the better will be staff compliance).

6. A school dietitian, if available, could serve as in-house coordinator of nutrition advice and change. Such changes would include agreed-upon items permitted in the teacher-exclusive areas of the school.

7. A food service director can provide information on food presentation and healthy choice changes in cafeteria meal menus for students and teachers, as well as in-house marketing of healthy choices. The food service director is another reasonable choice for in-house coordinator of nutrition advice and change. Most often, these individuals are housed in the central office of school districts, but you should never fail to call and ask for assistance.

8. Select, as a team member, a food vendor representative for cafeteria and vending services offered at school. This prospective member will have insights about alternative choices for healthy foods at discounted prices and possibly provide marketing support for any new healthy additions. Don't miss an opportunity to ask for aid from outside sources that may agree to assist financially or provide human resources to your school. This is especially true if the source specializes in an area included in your plan. This support may come from interested organizations that are not necessarily part of your planning/implementation team, so be global in your thought process. Don't forget private organizations and companies that may have similar goals and interests.

9. A Department of Public Health representative should be invited as a team member. The health department should be helpful—either indirectly, with existing resources from other projects

in your community, or directly, as a team member—and provide leadership in procuring government-funded health instructional tools that can be used in your faculty and staff school health promotion program. In fact, these individuals may help you qualify for grant money available for health promotion in your region, state, or local community.

10. As the leader of your school, you are most capable of finding additional individuals with appropriate expertise in needed areas that may serve your teams. Be sure to limit the number of team members. Avoid negatively impacting the group and suppressing the spontaneity and enthusiasm of members if the group becomes too large. The leadership team should decide on the number of team members and the needed representatives from the appropriate areas. As always, you may find the appropriate individuals to meet your needs in unusual places. Ad hoc support may come from nutritional education or training programs available in your area. School Health Coordinators or someone from the local WIC program may provide help.

4.2. The principal's plan for students' improved healthy weight and exercise should be a team approach.

You can relieve much of the pressure from teachers by reminding them that they are not expected to bear the entire burden of the nutritional or physical activities education of the students they teach. As a seasoned school leader, you have learned that, to best support your teachers, changes in the school culture must occur. As with any academic area, empower parents and local community members to be more active in the nutritional and exercise health of their children by increasing the awareness of the goals you have planned for the children in your school. One major role that teachers provide is exposing students to enough content knowledge and the related skills for success and holding students responsible to make appropriate, responsible, and healthy choices.

Teaching students choices can be achieved in several ways at various levels. Addition of nutritional and physical fitness knowledge may best be served when students have some input into the delivery process. We encourage a team approach with students, which promotes (a) a child-centered approach guided by direct and indirect classroom instruction on the concepts of healthy eating and (b) sustained changes in the school environment as outlined in the *Guidelines for School Health Programs to Promote Lifelong Healthy Eating* (CDC, 1996). We strongly recommend embedding both nutrition and physical content into the instructional process for all subject and content areas. Our direct experience is with schools that have been extremely successful using a content- and activity-embedded approach that is easily integrated as part of the instructional process. Furthermore, this approach actually helps improve the content delivery of any academic area, thus relieving teachers of having to find or plan many different lessons that take time to structure and implement successfully.

Each principal must provide teachers with assistance in incorporating any additional content or methodologies with integrated approaches that will personally motivate not only the students but also the classroom teacher. We urge you to search for appropriate materials, books, and other staff development tools to better prepare your teachers in this area. We invite you and your teachers to visit our Web site to share materials and ideas that work well with students. You are welcome to visit our site at www.impactchildhoodobesity.org. This Web site is continually updated and interactive; in addition, it provides lists of current and forthcoming books for teachers.

> "As long as you have a plan and a strong willingness to modify it as needed, you improve your odds for success greatly."

Perhaps you do not or cannot integrate a full plan at your school at this time. We urge you to work with your faculty and start slowly in introducing material into the instructional program. As long as you have a plan and a strong willingness to modify it as needed, you improve your odds for success greatly.

The *Guidelines for School Health Programs to Promote Lifelong Healthy Eating* (CDC, 1996) states that school health programs can help children and adolescents attain full educational potential and good health by providing them with the skills, social support, and environmental reinforcement they need to adopt long-term healthy eating behaviors. The U.S. Department of Agriculture's Nutrition Education and Training Program reinforces the message that eating habits influence the potential for learning as well as good health. Your students are not unaware of the importance of healthy eating. One would have to live in a vacuum to have missed that ever-playing message. But information is not application, and information alone does not provide the tools to turn knowledge into action nor help students recognize the importance for them. As you have probably experienced, sorting out sound nutrition and exercise advice from so much information prevalent in all media outlets can be more confusing than helpful. The school experience can play a vital role here. It is a significant positive when student education in nutrition and exercise at school can potentially have a direct influence on increased learning potential in all subject and multiple intelligences areas. Such an observed response should be a joy to every educator.

A team approach similar to the faculty plan is necessary to improve on or protect against unhealthy weight and the significant lack of exercise of your students. The goals for both teams are similar, as is the structure of the teams, but the differences are obvious. The information and the educational approach for your students must be grade-level specific and developmentally appropriate. The instructional plan must be motivational enough to answer the student question, "What's in it for me?"

Student input at the team level is important. How to include student leaders and student organizations will be unique to each school. Use student teams to provide data for what you need to have implemented. They will talk of relevance. As principal, you must not only think relevance but also necessity.

Modeling is perhaps the best instructional method of all time. Students will learn better when teachers are an example for them. Your faculty health promotion plan should facilitate this as one of its outcomes. Both plans can begin at the onset of the academic year or at midyear. Since the school day represents only a part of the life of your students, the more consistent the message on campus, the more the potential impact felt by each student. Half of your students eat one of their meals a day at school, and one in ten eats two meals a day a school. The school environment, from cafeteria options to vending machine choices, and from classroom education and training to physical education, free time, snack time, and class parties, provides teaching or reinforcing opportunities for the betterment of your students.

It is important that you stay aware of the various laws and policies that have been or will be coming into effect soon. For example, schools must respond to the $16 billion Child Nutrition Act of 2004 included within the National School Lunch Program. Many schools missed the deadline of July 1, 2006, which required the design and development of wellness policies signed into law in 2004. Each district must have a policy that includes (a) goals for nutrition education, (b) the specific nutritional guidelines for all food and drinks on each campus, and (c) plans to build a program to incorporate physical activity into each classroom. Many national and regional agencies provide materials or guidance in specific areas. Don't forget state and district agencies that can as well.

In previous chapters, we discussed the challenge of what is served at school-sponsored events, from sports and fun-time celebrations, to school fundraisers. Healthy food choices need not be boring or significantly different from what students are used to. Burgers are not bad, but serving grilled chicken sandwiches is healthier. Baked chips are better than French fries. Hot dogs made from chicken or soy protein taste good with the usual mustard, ketchup, and relish condiments at the school spring fair. Low-fat ice cream can cut calories in half and still taste good at a school ballgame. Exposure to such choices is in line with other positive daily messages, direct and subtle, that students could receive during the school day.

Help in such messaging can come from your school art department or classroom teachers and be created by your students. Tuned-in teachers can creatively incorporate such projects into the academic day. Such homegrown visual aids can make a better impact on your students than the slickest Madison Avenue advertisements. School pride is infectious. Principals should encourage classroom teachers, school nurses, physical education teachers, coaches, and the food service director to post positive, attractive nutrition and exercise messages in the classrooms, nursing station, gymnasium, and cafeteria. One of the most useful tools that a principal can use to help teachers incorporate content in nutrition and

> "Principals should encourage classroom teachers, school nurses, physical education teachers, coaches, and the food service director to post positive, attractive nutrition and exercise messages in the classrooms, nursing station, gymnasium, and cafeteria."

physical fitness is the integrated unit. Teachers will feel reluctant to do additional units or lessons on these topics, but when shown how to integrate their regular units with these additions, teachers will adopt this approach without much resistance.

Integrating Health and Wellness Into Classroom Instruction

Educational systems in the past have placed more emphasis on teaching the academic disciplines as unique, separate entities. This becomes especially true past third grade. However, the challenge continues in the new century to integrate the subject content for a greater holistic approach. The focus on high-stakes testing from a variety of sources has required teachers to focus on basic skills and lower level knowledge in the specific subject areas or academic disciplines, thus creating a learning environment that can be fragmented and irrelevant from the student's perspective. Many teachers are eager to correlate or even integrate content from other discipline areas but are uncertain of the steps needed for the process. Most important for our purposes here is the integration of nutritional content and physical activities into ANY subject area. The unit may be social studies with nutrition integrated or it may also have math, music, and so on, included. In our book, teachers can learn how to integrate content from one or more academic areas into thematic or integrated units. Our purpose is to show how to integrate nutrition and physical activities within the major content area.

Remember: If students are to truly learn and see the material they are studying as authentic, it must be relevant to their lives. An integrated unit is one that promises students will be personally engaged in their learning while bringing a much greater motivational appeal to the students.

Integrated units are more likely though to be taught in the classrooms of early childhood educators. Preschool and kindergarten teachers routinely plan their instructional patterns around central themes. However, integrated units are now becoming a vital part of elementary and middle school programs. Such units can be found in high school classrooms usually more in the form of correlated studies such as a history teacher and an English teacher planning a unit together on the Civil War integrating within separate classes the historical facts with writers of the period. Purchase such forthcoming books as *Overcoming Childhood Obesity: An Instructional Guide for Elementary Classroom Teachers; Overcoming Obesity for the Emerging Adolescent: An Instructional Guide for Middle School Teachers;* and *Overcoming Obesity in Adolescence: An Instructional Guide for High School* to list a few.

The Integrated Unit

When an integrated unit is taught, it is usually organized around a central theme. Students investigate using as many of the differing disciplines as they can in order to assist them in their inquiry. Themes can vary greatly and tend to be very broad. It is the teacher's responsibility to listen to the needs and interests of his or her students in order to choose a central theme that will be relevant and interesting to that particular age group. Possible themes include: space, family, change, environment, flying, dinosaurs, relationships, etc. Examples of more comprehensive themes to be examined by older students are multiple aspects of geography, different biomes, the Civil War, etc. In thematic studies, students have the opportunity to observe connections and relationships among the various disciplines that teachers have chosen to integrate into each particular unit. Teachers can easily implement the required standards and specific competencies within an integrated unit.

After a topic or theme has been selected, the teacher can then guide the planning process to integrate different concepts from other disciplines into the unit. The teacher points out the relationship of the different subjects to show students how all the subjects work together to accomplish a specific objective.

Every integrated unit should have a rationale for implementation. Students need to know the reason and importance of the unit they will be studying. Students need to understand how the theme they are studying relates to the whole picture. The rationale can answer questions such as: Why is this topic important? What difference will it make if I understand this topic? How will I use this information? It is important that the topic being taught is relevant to the students and that the students see and understand this relevance.

The unit objective is an important component in planning for a successful integrated unit. Unit objectives can be broken down into two categories. First, there are the large focus areas to be accomplished, which the authors call the major expectations. These can also be referred to as the overall unit goals. They focus the purpose of the entire unit of work. These objectives state the major expectations the teacher has for students upon completion of the unit.

A second type of objective is content or process, also known as a main objective. Main objectives are the short-term objectives included in a single lesson. These objectives provide a measure by which the teacher can assess the effectiveness of instruction. This type of objective usually follows a behavioral format and answers one of the following questions: Whom? What? Under what conditions? How well? This objective explains what the student is to learn from each particular lesson. This objective also states what is to be mastered through the main activities in the unit.

Establishing objectives and making the students aware of these objectives are important in planning a successful integrated unit. Objectives allow the teacher and the students to remain focused during the unit. Objectives tell the students what they will be held responsible for and what they will be evaluated on. They are important in allowing the activities and lesson to further understanding in specific, established areas. The teacher must make sure that the objectives are stated clearly and are thoroughly understood by all students before beginning the unit.

In the initial unit design, only one fully developed lesson plan is necessary. This lesson plan will be the one used to introduce the unit. It should be planned with a related concept or question (anticipatory set) to orient the students to the theme and allow them to become excited and enthusiastic about the material they will be studying. This initial lesson will help students to begin responding to the unit theme.

When developing each lesson within the integrated unit, the teacher should include statements of the skills and/or knowledge to be emphasized, how this learning is relevant to students, and what students will know or be able to do as a result of participation in the lesson. Complete lesson plans can be prepared from these descriptions. In writing an integrated unit plan design, it is important that the teacher have specific objectives allowing different cognitive levels to be reached. Sometimes a teacher can design an integrated unit plan by using a web that suggests some possible lessons relating to a particular theme the students will study.

Coding procedures are used in order to organize the main objectives with the enabling activities. These coding procedures are determined by the teacher or group of teachers according to what works best for them. Use of coding procedures saves the teacher time and keeps planning organized and consistent. Task analysis is used to show the individual tasks that students will be performing throughout the units. Tasks can be organized in the form of a web map or another preferred form. Examples of both coding procedures and task analysis are given in the sample integrated unit on biomes that appears below.

The enabling activities are the actual experiences students complete to learn the content, which has been determined by the main objectives. This includes the specific content and the methods used (discussion, inquiry, cooperative learning, discovery, and so on).

At the end of the unit, students and teacher should evaluate the entire unit. This helps the teachers know what was and what was not successful in the unit. The successful activities can be used again. Those that were not as successful should be modified or discarded. The teacher can learn a lot from the comments of the students. Sometimes the theme of the unit is not relevant to students and, therefore, students are unable to relate to the topic. Other times, the problem is in the way a particular lesson is presented. Whatever the comments, it is important for the teacher to be aware of the pros and cons of using this unit again.

Sample Integrated Unit on Biomes for Fifth Grade

Major Expectation

By the end of the unit, fifth grade students will be able to master skills in the area of science plus skills in computers, art, communication, history, geography, nutrition, math, and language arts to research and describe a specific biome.

Unit Rationale

This unit concentrates on the study of biomes. It is an integrated unit designed for fifth grade students. The unit is designed to incorporate computer skills, art skills, language arts skills, speech and communication skills, history skills, geography skills, nutrition and cooking skills, as well as the science information necessary to develop a unit on biomes. The enabling activities will also allow students to develop their social skills as they work together to research and present their designated biomes. Students will also begin to develop an appreciation for differing environments in the world. The purpose of this unit goes beyond learning the mere characteristics of biomes. It is designed to create a wider knowledge base and an appreciation of specific geographical areas.

Enabling Activities

The teacher will

1. review relevant concepts and terms: climate, temperature, rainfall, and organisms.
2. assign people to groups: four people per group.
3. assign each group a different aspect of the biomes.
4. instruct students to use Microsoft PowerPoint or other software to develop a presentation.

Each group will

1. research their particular topic.
2. take notes on their particular topic.
3. make a bibliography from the books they used (APA format).
4. design a computer presentation in PowerPoint.
    a. design seven slides (minimum)
    b. add graphics (clip art)
    c. add notes
    d. add transitions, timing
    e. add graphs, map, and chart, with necessary data

5. make a costume for their presentation topic and come dressed for presentation in their costume.

6. make a map of the world, indicating where their team's biome is located.

7. write a final paper, three to five pages not including the bibliography page (correct spelling and grammar; type final paper on a word processor; present final presentation as a group—must be five to seven minutes long). Students will need to show their group's PowerPoint presentation, describe their biome, dress in their costumes and add props, if necessary. By the end of their presentation, all students should be able to demonstrate their knowledge on the different aspects of biomes. A creative essay test will be given at the end of the unit.

Student Assessment

(All assessments will be based upon related rubrics scored by the individual, group members, class members, and the teacher—a portfolio could also be used if so desired.) Traditional quizzes and a unit exam may be used at the discretion of the teacher.

- Language Arts: Group grade
- Language Arts: Presentation grade
- Language Arts: Research paper grade
- Arts: Props and costume grade
- Nutrition grade
- Computer: Graphics and slides grade
- Science: Creative essay test grade. (Teacher and Individual Student Only)

Main Objectives

Arts (A)

A-1: Students will make a costume and/or props to add to their presentation. All members of the group must make a costume to represent their biome (for example, a cactus living in the desert).

A-2: Students will draw a map showing where the biomes of the world are located.

Affective/Social (AS)

AS-1: Students will exhibit a positive attitude toward scientific inquiry as a way of thinking and problem solving.

AS-2: Students will show curiosity, inventiveness, and critical thinking.

AS-3: Students will develop an appreciation for the struggles of early settlers in adapting to the biome they are studying.

AS-4: Students will be able to work in groups, each contributing a particular task to communicate the information they obtained (for example, the group secretary will type the final paper for the group).

Computer/Keyboarding (C)

C-1: Students will be able to work in PowerPoint in order to create a minimum of seven slides showing the different characteristics of their biomes.

C-2: Students will type the final copies of their papers on a word processor.

Nutrition (N)

N-1: Students will be able to experiment with preparing foods with ingredients from their particular biome. This will be incorporated into their presentation.

N-2: Students will be able to label each food group based upon the new food group pyramid for their biome.

Geography (G)

G-1: Students will be able to identify on a map of the world where their particular biome is located.

G-2: Students will be able to identify the effects of the physical environment on their biome.

Language Arts (LA)

LA-1: Students will be able to demonstrate the ability to communicate through the writing of journals.

LA-2: Students will be able to use the media center and computer lab to research their designated biome.

LA-3: Students will write a three- to five-page paper using description to show the reader their biome.

LA-4: Students will write a bibliography to show at least five of the resources they used to gather their information.

LA-5: Students will be able to use speaking skills they previously learned when speaking in front of groups.

Math (M)

M-1: Students will be able to interpret given data from a graph.

M-2: Students will be able to construct a graph from data given to them, showing the number of specific populations of plants and animals that live in the area they are researching.

Science (S)

S-1: Students will be able to gain insights about the effect of climate and weather on plant and animal life in differing biomes around the world.

S-2: Students will demonstrate the ability to "list" plants and animals in a particular area.

S-3: Students will be able to list specific biomes of the earth and give at least three characteristics of each biome.

S-4: Students will demonstrate the ability to describe observations and data through spoken and written words, graphs, drawings, diagrams, maps, and/or mathematical equations.

S-5: Students will exhibit a positive attitude toward scientific inquiry as a way of thinking and problem solving.

S-6: Students will be able to compare and contrast different characteristics of different biomes.

Speech and Communications (SC)

SC-1: Students will be able to use speaking skills to develop a five-minute presentation on their particular biomes.

The teacher will now be able to implement the lessons of the unit by incorporating activities using specific objectives from the different subject areas listed above. The objectives are now coded for easy integration.

Week 1: Monday–Friday

Main Objectives

AS-1, AS-2, AS-3, AS-4, C-2, G-1, N-1, LA-2, LA-4, S-1, S-2, S-3, S-5

Presentation

Students will be asked if they have ever been to a different area of the world, such as a desert or a rainforest. Those that have will be asked to describe what they saw. If nobody volunteers, or no one has ever been, the teacher will ask students to imagine what it would be like. The teacher will write the words they use on the board. The teacher will then explain to the students that they will be learning about different biomes. The teacher will give definitions of biomes and review the meanings of words they have previously studied: climate, temperature, rainfall, plant and animal life, environment, and physical properties. Specific food sources available will be included. The teacher will explain that all of these help to describe biomes. Students will take notes in their notebooks already specified for the unit on biomes.

Enabling Activity

The teacher will divide the class into groups of four by having them draw cards from a desk. Once the groups have formed, the teacher will assign each group a different biome. Each member will be given a specific task, and the group as a whole will choose a team name that describes their biome. (For example, the Cereus Cacti Team is named for a cactus that grows in the desert.) Once they have a designated name for their team, the competition between teams begins. They can make logos and banners for their team—whatever they choose to help excite their team. The class will then go to the media center to research their particular biome. They will use books, encyclopedias, magazines, computers, and atlases. The resources they will choose from will be lengthy.

The teacher will also have a list of books on reserve for the students to use. Each group will need to take notes on note cards.

Closure

After the class has completed the research on their biomes and has taken all the notes they need, each group will type a bibliography, using APA format. The bibliography must contain a minimum of five sources. One must be a magazine article. One must be a book. One must be from the Internet. The other two can be from sources that they choose. The groups will turn in their bibliography and note cards on Friday.

Student Assessment

- Each group will write a bibliography.
- Each group will turn in note cards, organized and titled.
- Each group will turn in a logo/banner with their team name and mission statement.
- Each team will be monitored throughout by the teacher and other members of their group.

There will be a chart for each group with members' names showing the objectives of each member checked off when completed. A space for comments will also be beside each child's name.

Materials

Poster board

Encyclopedias

Pens and crayons

Index cards

Materials on reserve in the media center

Rulers

Week 2: Monday–Friday

Main Objectives

AS-1, AS-2, AS-4, C-1, LA-1, LA-2, M-1, M-2, S-2, S-3, S-4

Presentation

Each member of each team will begin by writing in their journal. They will write all that they can remember about the biome they researched. They will not be allowed to talk to other members of their group when they do this. The teacher will then explain that they will be going to the computer lab to learn about PowerPoint. The teacher will explain that by the end of the unit each group will develop and present a five-minute presentation to their class. He or she will explain that PowerPoint allows them to make slides and that these slides will be used to make up the bulk of their presentation. Once the groups are in the computer lab, the teacher will walk through and explain PowerPoint to the students. The teacher will explain how to make slides, how to use transitions, how to add graphics, how to add graphs and charts, how to add clip art, how to change color, and how to make a slide show.

Enabling Activity

After the teacher has thoroughly explained this information, students will be given time to explore PowerPoint on their own. Then each group will type in the information they got from their research. They will incorporate clip art showing their biomes, make transitions, and add color. Each group will have a minimum of seven slides to use in their presentation. One slide will include available food sources from the area that the students will place inside the new food pyramid.

Closure

At the end of the week, PowerPoint will be reviewed, and grammar and spelling will be checked on slides.

Student Assessment

- Students will be continuously monitored as they work on the computer.
- Students will turn in their disk twice—once on Wednesday and for a final time on Thursday.
- Group teams will again check off objectives when they are done and make comments on all group members of their team.
- Journals will be checked to see if they are completed.

Materials

Research cards students have completed

Disks

Computers with Microsoft PowerPoint

Journals

Week 3: Monday–Friday

Main Objectives

A-1, A-2, AS-1, AS-2, AS-4, C-2, N-1, N-2, G-1, LA-1, LA-2, S-1, S-4

Presentation

The teacher will begin again by having each student write in their journal to comment on how they felt about using PowerPoint to make slides and show their information. Once journals are completed, the teacher will explain that this week they are going to continue to work towards their presentation. The teacher will explain that each group will turn in a three- to five-page paper typed and completed by the end of the week. This paper should be written from the research they obtained and the insight they have gained on their biome. The teacher will explain that this week will also be used to implement other disciplines to enhance their presentations.

Enabling Activities

Each student will be able to design his or her own costume to represent something from their biome. The costume may be that of a plant or animal living in their biome. They are to decorate these costumes using any of the art supplies available. They are to wear their costumes to their presentations. Students will also be drawing a map of the world and highlighting where their particular biome is located. Finally, students may choose between using some ingredients that are found in their biome (for example, spices found in the rainforest) to cook something to share in their presentation and find some music to play during their presentation that represents sounds from their biome (for example, sounds of raindrops falling). Additionally, the students will list the foods from the different biomes and demonstrate these under the new food pyramid.

Closure

At the end of the week, students should have their presentations ready to present. A three- to five-page paper should be written and typed on a word processor.

Student Assessment

- Groups will be continuously monitored.
- Journals will be checked and read.
- Group teams will check objectives and write comments, as will the teacher.
- A two- to five-page paper will be checked for content, grammar, spelling, and length.

Materials

Art supplies: glitter, glue, scissors, tape, and markers

Audiotapes and player

Cooking supplies

Computer/word processor

Week 4: Monday–Friday

Main Objectives

AS-1, AS-2, AS-4, C-1, G-1, G-2, N-1, N-2, LA-1, LA-5, M-1, S-1, S-2, S-3, S-4, S-5

Presentation

Students will begin the week by commenting in their journals how they have liked working in groups, the theme, the activities, and the art work done last week. After journals have been completed, the class will begin its biome kickoff. Each team will hang their banner or poster. Students will sample the foods from the various biomes and determine the nutritional value. Students will have a twenty-minute pep rally before their presentations. Students will be dressed in their costumes. The best costume will be voted on, and the winner will receive a small prize or certificate.

Enabling Activity

The teacher will have the room set up with a computer and a big screen to show students' PowerPoint presentations. Each group will present their five-minute presentation and will show their slides and explain their costumes and props.

Closure

The teacher will have each group review the highlights of all their biomes and will have students take notes in their biome notebooks. If information is missing, the teacher will add it in conversation so students will have it in their notebooks. The class will take a final test on the information covered by the students and teachers in the biome unit.

Student Assessment

- Students will receive a team grade on their presentation as well as an individual grade.
- Students will have a written test (or evaluations based on the content using a final rubric) on the information covered during the unit.

Materials

Students' disks

Computers with Microsoft PowerPoint

Students' props

Big screen to show slides

Unit Evaluation

Arts

- Costume design—creativity and detail
- Map of the world with correct location of biome

Computer/Keyboarding

- PowerPoint clip art, transition, color, seven slides, graph
- Final paper typed on word processor

Language Arts

- Group grade on paper—grammar, spelling, content
- Individual contribution—comments by teacher and students
- Bibliography—five sources, APA format
- Journals

Math

- Chart or graph showing population of plants and animals

Science/Geography/History

- Evaluated by unit test

Nutrition

- Evaluated by rubric measuring selection of food chosen from the biomes and an analysis of the nutritional value of the food based upon the new food pyramid and the nutritional guide on the package of selected foods.

Speech and Communications

- Speaking techniques, posture, confidence

Additional Resources

As principal, you may want to locate relevant materials for teachers that have numerous units and lessons that have been tested and used with students in real school settings. Many lessons or ideas for lessons are available from local agencies. Some states also provide lesson ideas for teaching nutrition and physical fitness inside and outside of the classroom.

The North Carolina State Board of Education has created a Healthy Active Children Policy, starting with the 2006–2007 school year, designed to raise the activity level for K–5 students to include 20 minutes of physical activity each day during normal classroom hours and 45 minutes of physical activity for Grades 6–8. To encourage healthy, active lifestyles for our students, the lessons include both indoor and outdoor activities in a variety of settings. Most of the activities are employed with integration to other subject areas to foster transference of course objectives.

Plenty of advice is available free from government agencies and professional organizations. The following locations may provide valuable tools, especially since time is an enemy to all teachers. This list comes from the CDC's *Guidelines for School Health Programs to Promote Lifelong Healthy Eating*. These sources can provide nutrition education curricula material in print, audiovisual, and computer-based formats. You can use these to help you identify what may be helpful for your school.

1. Food and Nutrition Information Center, National Agricultural Library, U.S. Department of Agriculture, 10301 Baltimore Blvd., Room 304, Beltsville, MD 20705

2. National Food Service Management Institute, PO Box 188, University of Mississippi, University, MS 38667

3. American Dietetic Association, National Center for Nutrition and Dietetics, 216 W. Jackson Blvd., Suite 800, Chicago, IL 60606-6995

4. American Heart Association, 7272 Greenville Ave., Dallas, TX 75231-4596

5. American School Food Services Association, 1600 Duke St., 7th Floor, Alexandria, VA 22314

6. Consumer Information Center, Pueblo, CO 81009

7. American Cancer Society, 1599 Clifton Road, N.E., Atlanta, GA 30329

8. International Food Information Council, 1100 Connecticut Ave., N.W., Suite 430, Washington, DC 20036

9. National Heart, Lung and Blood Institute Information Center, PO Box 30105, Bethesda, MD 20824-0105

10. Team Nutrition, U.S. Department of Agriculture, 3101 Park Center Drive, Room 802, Alexandria, VA 22302

Possible Roadblocks

Students may not always need to be given choices, but changes may be met with resistance. As a principal, you are trained to deal with resistance.

This case history emphasizes a nutrition change conflict: A parent in one school that we assisted complained to the teacher that since children were no longer allowed to get second portions at lunch (not a frequent school cafeteria option nationally), her son was not getting enough food at school. It took an understanding principal to explain that all school meals are based on government-specified healthy choices and that school-age appropriate total lunch calories are made available to all students. That message is now better disseminated to parents.

To champion this task, you need to understand that there are no proven road maps with outcome data for you to fall back on. The best approach may be your approach, since success to date has been limited. Limited success may have been the product of a school faculty and staff that had not been educated enough to see the value. Limited success could have occurred by not soliciting input from school personnel, students, and others. A plan not well designed, one that does not include input from thought leaders who have the expertise to encourage, support, and enhance a plan, is a formula for non-implementation. Such shortsightedness dooms many a good idea.

The principal's job here is to rally the faculty and staff to your cause. Go beyond the obvious. There are changes in cafeteria meals and available snacks during the school day that every principal should be making. You will have to do this type of change anyway or risk having it done to you by your superintendent or the state; such changes are rapidly being adopted nationwide. These changes, however, do not alter the habits of your staff or your students; they only delay bad habits to another time of day. Changes made must promote personal change. Teaching is all about making students think and grow in their thought process. Your plan must encompass that to be successful.

The CDC's *Guidelines for School Health Programs to Promote Lifelong Healthy Eating* (1996) gives you a strong basis for implementing a plan for your school. Published medical and psychological research, using evidence-based research, recognize that school programs, if they include a better emphasis on health in the school curriculum, allow elementary, middle school, and high school students to reach their full academic potential. Remember, schools are now required to provide nutritional education from preschool to 12th grade. The goal is lofty and results are slow in coming. The majority of U.S. schools are far from attaining even part of this multifactorial goal. The U.S. Department of Agriculture Nutrition Education and Training Programs are far behind their goal for nutrition education to be a major offering in all schools by the year 2000. We suggest that as the instructional leader of the school, you find ways to make this happen and give teachers the freedom to experiment to find the best approaches that work for them. Now, let's build a wellness plan for students!

Principal's Team for Student Improved Healthy Weight and Exercise

Mission: To establish reasonable healthy weight change priorities for students at school, compatible with age- and grade-level student academic requirements.

Depending on how comprehensive a principal wants this plan to be, it can be implemented in stages.

Team member suggestions:

1. Teachers should be selected from each grade level to act as team leaders for their grade.

2. School nurses, if available, can be a resource for nutrition and healthy weight information for classroom use.

3. Local hospital administrators could supply dieticians, nurses, and student teachers to assist in your school needs plan.

4. A physical education instructor can provide advice on maximizing activities in physical education classes with emphasis on having fun, on building student confidence in doing exercise outside of PE class, and in skill training. He or she can provide advice for teachers on structured and unstructured exercise for classroom and recess times. Physical education instructors can help students make the connection between healthy eating and exercise.

5. A food service director can help teachers reinforce healthy food option changes made in the cafeteria and provide nutrition

teaching aid tips for classroom use. Attractiveness of healthy food options affects choices and should be a goal of the food service director. Menu options for parents to inform them of best choices bring the family into the mix. This also could be a role for the food service director.

6. Student representatives from all grade levels, student government members, or club leaders can provide student input for age group relevance.

7. A parent PTA representative can act as liaison to the parent-school organization to help propagate information on healthy eating and exercise to parents. This will help create the continuity needed for successful behavior changes that teachers will be teaching.

8. A food vendor representative may be able to help with practical information, education, other support tools, and handouts to students and their parents.

9. The school newspaper faculty advisor and student members can use the in-school media to publicize the goals and create legitimacy for the program.

10. The school counselor can act as a reinforcer when counseling students.

11. An administrative representative as liaison to the principal should be included.

12. A Web site manager can be invited to help develop a school instructional Web site with links to legitimate resources for teachers, nurses, PE teachers, dietitians, and so forth.

The principal needs to facilitate and define what data measurements are worthwhile to collect to give students, faculty, and parents a visual or mathematical gauge of the starting point and progress of the plan to improve student healthy weight. Keep in mind that prevention of abnormal weight gain or further unhealthy weight gain in those at an unhealthy weight is progress.

Student Unhealthy Weight Actions

1. Define unhealthy weight in all students in the school using BMI as the measurement.

2. Establish how, when, where, and who will record BMI for each student. Ideally, it should be done at the onset and end of each school year in the school nursing station. It does not require a nurse to measure height and weight; a student's BMI can be read from a standard chart. Such charts are available in every pediatrician's office and can also be found on the CDC Web site; that government organization allows them to be reproduced. As you know from earlier in this chapter, a student's BMI needs to be correlated with the age- and sex-specific numbers to determine the percentile of BMI category. Overweight in children and adolescence is identified as the 95th percentile and higher for age and sex.

3. Decide how to explain and then disseminate BMI information to students and parents or other caregivers.

4. Provide information to parents on what your school is doing to increase nutrition education.

5. Provide information to parents on what your school is doing to increase physical activity opportunities at school.

6. Invite parents to follow the same nutrition and exercise advice at home.

7. Recommend primary care physician consultation for students determined to be at the BMI 95th percentile or greater if a letter is to be sent home to parents with this information.

8. Do not provide specific advice. All specific recommendations should come from the primary care physician for at-risk students.

9. Periodic information on nutrition and exercise could be sent home with the student for family use. Such information would come from the lesson plan used by your teachers.

4.3. Unhealthy weight impacts the emotional-social development of students. To address it, you need to better understand it.

Overweight children and adolescents are victims of teasing, bullying, and prejudice and thus tend to have a lower self-esteem than predicted. The school environment is a breeding ground for such actions and trains those of unhealthy weight in the art of self-protection, isolation, and defensive behaviors. Some such behaviors are external, while others are internal psychological adaptations that may not be healthy.

Low self-esteem is common in children and adolescents in general. It is usually higher in the younger ages and decreases toward adolescence. Low self-esteem, on the other hand, is more common in overweight adolescents. As a compensation for low self-esteem, overweight teens are likely to choose friends who tend to be either younger or older. Both groups are less critical and less judgmental toward them. The power of your teacher education and role modeling has the potential to alter the social response of at-risk students.

The adolescent years are fertile grounds for the development of personal goals and expectations that may be somewhat distorted or delayed by a deflated self-esteem—or enhanced by positive behavior changes. In overweight youth, dealing with the social issues associated with being overweight may significantly improve their quality of life.

Overweight and depression do not necessarily have a cause-and-effect relationship, but when they occur together, they are hard to separate out as to what is affecting the other more. If depression is suspected as a significant factor, help needs to come from a mental health care professional. School is not a place to assess or provide treatment for depression.

Be aware that there may be saboteurs of your plan in your school. The most likely candidates may be prejudiced teachers or those who are resistant to change. Students, school administrators, physical education teachers, and other school personnel are potential saboteurs due to prejudice against those of unhealthy weight.

Hopefully, teachers and other school staff involved in the faculty wellness plan will be in the process of being deprogrammed. If a weight prejudice problem exists with staff, it is the job of the principal to address it directly. The following case history demonstrates the effects of discrimination.

Obesity in Childhood Can Lead to Disruptive Behavior at School: A Case History

A 12-year-old overweight girl, who had been bullied by fellow students, became the aggressor and caused disruption in the classroom on multiple occasions. The teacher's response was to restore order in the classroom by giving the girl detention. For this young girl, going on the offensive was the only response she could come up with. The effect was punishment and further isolation from classmates and teachers. With no guidance, insight, or understanding to help her, she became a repeat offender. Her parents eventually transferred her to another school. This was the second time in two years that her school was changed for disciplinary reasons, and she had the label of troublemaker. The following year, her parents transferred her to a private school. Her disciplinary issues may not have been as severe if the situation had been better understood or had been addressed by the teachers, the principal, and her parents. Time spent on her discipline could have been channeled into constructive behavior changes if the issue of weight prejudice could have been identified. It appears it was easier to discipline rather than evaluate in this particular situation. Would it have gone the same way and to the same end if it had not been an overweight child? Would there have been more questions as to the root of this girl's anger if she looked different? We are not sure of the answer. How can your teachers avoid situations similar to this case?

Overweight children can appear years older than their chronological age. Unsuspecting adults may expect unrealistic responses from children who are younger than they look. When children do not understand what an adult is asking or are unable to comply because the request is beyond their age-related experience, it can give them grave personal doubts about their abilities. These children are made to feel inadequate, and thus they display even less self-confidence and are more unsure of themselves. When youngsters have experienced misunderstandings with adults, they anticipate having further problems with adults. It is not difficult to see how these problems begin: being misunderstood by others because your size makes you look older than you really are can lead to weight-related disruptive behaviors. The

Figure 4.1   Precentage of Young People Who Are Overweight

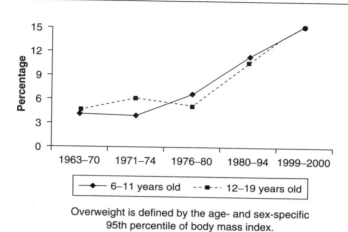

Overweight is defined by the age- and sex-specific
95th percentile of body mass index.

SOURCE: National Center for Chronic Disease Prevention and Health Promotion (n.d.); data from American Psychiatric Association (2000).

Figure 4.2   Percent of Children and Adolescents Who Meet U.S. Dietary Guidelines, 1994–96, 1998

Guideline	6–11 years old		12–19 years old	
	Boys	Girls	Boys	Girls
Fat	31%	34%	30%	35%
Saturated Fat	25%	25%	28%	34%
Vegetables	18%	19%	33%	26%
Fruits	23%	24%	14%	18%

SOURCE: National Center for Chronic Disease Prevention and Health Promotion (n.d.); data from U.S. Department of Agriculture.

level of criticism from different sources makes these students vulnerable. Your job as principal is to educate teachers on the drawbacks of age misunderstanding. The CDC charts above may give you a sense of the problem.

The effect of unhealthy weight on academic achievement is clear. The CDC *Guidelines for School Health Programs To Promote Lifelong Healthy Eating* clearly state (1996, p. 3) that skipping breakfast can adversely affect children's performance in problem-solving tasks. Improvements in standardized test scores and decreased absenteeism and tardiness were shown in school break-fast participants as compared to students who qualified for the program but did not participate. A loss of continuity of learning through missed school days due to illness associated with being overweight must play a role here. Other issues are social and psychological ones that interfere with learning, such as a lack of self-confidence, teacher prejudice, peer discrimination, and non-acceptance into the group.

Unhealthy eating undermines expected growth and cognitive function. It promotes the development of many chronic diseases, as we have discussed, and weakens body response to infection.

A Rand Corporation study showed that increasing physical education in school by as little as an extra hour a week in female kindergarten and first grade students cuts overweight by as much as 10%. Well-constructed plans that fit the needs of students and teachers could lead to major changes in the way schools fight obesity. Based on study findings, it was estimated that increasing physical education to five hours a week could decrease the number of overweight girls in American schools in kindergarten and first grade by 43% and those at risk for being overweight by 60%. The Rand Corporation used the data collected by the U.S. Department of Education as part of a long-term assessment of 11,192 children who entered kindergarten in 1998 in about 1000 schools. The results released so far are only for those children's

> This book is providing you with a healthy weight road map to follow and the tools to help guide you toward implementing your school plan. Chances are that as many as 25% of your current students will benefit from these efforts. We estimate that more than nine million children and youth between the ages of 6 and 19 years are overweight.

kindergarten and first grade years (Datar, Strum, & Magnabosco, 2004). The research found that only 16% of kindergartners had daily physical education instruction and 13% had it either once a week or not at all. Study lead author Ashlesha Datar said, "While physical education often gets cut when education budgets are tight, it has a potentially important role in the battle against obesity" (p. 1505).

Dr. Vincent Ferrandino, executive director of the National Association of Elementary School Principals, (as reported by the U.S. Department of Agriculture) found most schools scaled back or eliminated recess time and physical education classes to provide more preparation time for student testing programs, a key part of the school-funded formulas. Many schools that made choices to cut back on PE classes now realize that it was not a good decision in regard to their students' health (U.S. Department of Agriculture, 2001).

"We must remember," says Dr. Brownell, "that physical activity increase is not going to compensate for the unhealthy diets kids are eating" (2004, p. 1237). Studies in the medical literature show modest reduction in the number of sugar-containing carbonated drinks to be associated with a reduction in the number of overweight and obese children (James, Thomas, Cavan, & Kerr, 2004).

Dr. Dietz, in *Policy Tools for the Childhood Obesity Epidemic* (Dietz, Bland, Gortmaker, Molloy, & Schmid, 2002), highlighted the fact that obesity is a giant when compared to other diseases and that 58 million people are living with serious health risks from obesity compared to 22 million with heart disease, 16 million with diabetes, 8 million with cancer, and 800,000 to 900,000 with HIV/AIDS. Dietz further implied that the contribution of obesity to other major killers of Americans, primarily heart disease, diabetes, and so forth, requires an increased emphasis on not only treatment but also prevention.

To reinforce our stated position, Surgeon General Satcher, in his *The Surgeon General's Call to Action to Prevent and Decrease Overweight and Obesity* (Department of Health and Human Services, 2001, Foreword), said that "many people believe that dealing with overweight and obesity is a personal problem. To some degree they are right, but it is also a community responsibility. When there are no safe, accessible places for children to play or adults to walk, jog, or ride a bike, that is a community

"Based on study findings, it was estimated that increasing physical education to five hours a week could decrease the number of overweight girls in American schools in kindergarten and first grade by 43% and those at risk for being overweight by 60%."

responsibility. When school lunchrooms or office cafeterias do not provide healthy and appealing food choices, that is a community responsibility. When we do not require daily physical education in our schools, that is a community problem." We firmly believe that as educational leaders, you can either leave these important decisions totally in the hands of your legislators and special interest groups or *be on the leading edge of an inevitable change.*

The potential future health care costs associated with pediatric obesity and its associated medial problems are staggering. The surgeon general predicted that preventable disease and death associated with obesity might exceed that associated with cigarette smoking. We have introduced you to multidisciplinary plan options that can work in your school and classrooms.

The rapid rise in childhood and adolescent overweight between 1970 and 2002, our most recent epidemiological data, can be explained mostly by a sedentary lifestyle and poor eating habit changes. The childhood overweight epidemic is complex in its causes and therefore needs to be addressed on multiple fronts. One important focal point is a modification of the school environment. Legislation at the state government level will continue to occur in some form. It is the enlightened school principal who knows best what is possible and functional for students. It is at the local school level that short-term and long-range decisions should be made. A principal needs to take the lead in determining the importance a healthier weight has on improved academic performance and improved sense of self-worth, as well as more functional social interaction that a healthier weight brings to overweight and non-overweight students alike.

The responsibility to change our childhood overweight culture is not completely in the hands of the schools, although there are those who would like it to be so. Historically, school has been an "imperfect panacea" for the ills of society. However, it is a fact that teachers remain some of the most important authority figures outside the home and thus can influence not only a child's learning ability but also can help direct what that child can do to help family members at home. This approach to help a student change eating and exercise for personal and family betterment worked successfully in smoking cessation campaigns in which children influenced their parents to stop smoking. Schools represent an environment for the delivery of interventions directed at unhealthy weight. Principals and teachers do not have to take this job on alone. In most communities, there are ways to engage willing health care professionals; dietitians; exercise and behavior specialists; local government, including departments of health; civic-minded businesses; the clergy; and the media to play active, visible roles.

CHAPTER FIVE

Maximizing Principal, Teacher, and Student Plans for Nutritional Improvement and Physical Fitness

In the previous four chapters, we have covered all of the major aspects related to what we believe is the Eighth Cardinal Principal discussed in Chapter 2. We have defined the principle as the intentional and active practice of preventing childhood obesity. If you have learned the enclosed content and implemented the plans and programs that we have suggested, you should have several major components in process:

1. Your own personal plan for improving your nutritional needs and physical fitness needs to advance your own health and to serve as a role model to teachers, parents, and students in your school.

2. Your school should have a faculty improvement plan for all adults working in the building that will provide an avenue for improving their nutritional needs and physical fitness needs in the workplace.

3. Your faculty should have the basic knowledge to design instructional units and lessons that are grade-appropriate and integrated by core subject areas that include nutritional and physical fitness content and activities that can guide students in making good nutritional choices. In addition, your school should provide direct physical education by certified professionals, and teachers should include indirect instructional activities that include some sustained movement and/or muscle resistance as embedded activities in all core and elective instructional areas.

4. Your plans should be guided by federal, state, and local mandates for providing a nutritionally safe and focused environment in all curricular and non-curricular activities under the aegis of the school. Appropriate individuals and groups from the community should be invited and encouraged to participate on boards and committees or to assist school personnel in the implementation process of all related laws and requirements.

5. Your nutritional, health, and physical fitness plans for you, additional school leaders, teachers, staff members, students, and even parents, if possible, should include some of the elements found in what has come to be known as wellness plans. The wellness plans can incorporate the elements of nutritional education and physical fitness but should go beyond these areas to include time and stress management. While we mentioned some of these latter elements throughout the book, additional resources should be found to learn more about selecting and managing priorities and the related stress issues.

All of these components can have a positive impact on overall health and can be helpful for advancing effective nutritional education and physical fitness for everyone involved.

MAKING THE GRADE

As principal of a school or other educational leader in a central office or state agency, you are most eager to see end-of-year test results of students in your school and/or school system. In fact, federal, state, and local government and nonprofit groups are grading schools, school systems, and states on the academic achievement outcomes of students. Equally important is the grade you would make in your plans above. After the first year, would you have made an A, B, or a lower grade? How would your school or school system be graded by the nonprofit group, the Center for Science in the Public Interest? Would you make a better grade than schools in your state or region?

Just released, the Center for Science in the Public Interest (2006), gave grades from the full range from A to F. While almost one-half of the states received the grade of F, several states fared much better. Kentucky received the highest grade with an A-, followed by Alabama, Arkansas, California and New Mexico with the grade of B+, and Arizona and Tennessee with the grade of B. The Center grades the nation's schools by states in such areas as the implementation and effectiveness of policies that govern nutritional standards for foods, including foods and beverages sold outside of the regular cafeteria, such as sodas and snacks sold in vending machines. The Center evaluates items sold for fundraisers and at school-related events. States receiving lower grades were faulted for lacking policies forbidding sports or fruit drinks, portion size limits, and sugary soft drinks at the high school level. Many of the states had policies for elementary schools but no formalized policies for middle schools and high schools. Most states have new polices for the 2006–2007 year, including those contained in the new federal law known as the Child Nutrition Act. We hope you did well; if not, implement the required policies and we know that you will earn an A at the end of next year. Visit our Web site for more information on the grading scale and procedures used by the Center for Science in the Public Interest.

BEYOND INSTRUCTIONAL LEADERSHIP

As we have previously stated, school principals and other educational leaders of the twenty-first century face overwhelming changes from national incentives and program reform down to bringing about sustained learning and change at the individual classroom level. In addition to facing the 60–80+ hour work week and undoable workload, insufficent compensation, and conflict with most stakeholder groups, the lack of the unknown and what you will face in the future can be major concerns now. While you may not be able to predict what are the next great reform efforts or what additional duties you will have to add to your already overloaded workload, you can be prepared to face the future with a physical body that is healthy and within the correct ranges for weight, height, and gender because you have mastered good nutritional habits and have participated in physical activities that have assisted you in meeting your weight goals and hopefully in avoiding serious obesity-related illnesses, and you have learned to deal with time and stress effectively. Equally important, you have been not only the instructional leader in your school but perhaps a life saver to a large population of your teachers and students by implementing, monitoring, and improving all of the plans we have discussed in the book.

A PERSONAL WORD ABOUT YOUR HEALTH AND STRESS

Stress is a major part of life. Everyone experiences it in some form daily and each individual reacts differently. This new role of being the leader for addressing this new epidemic will be stressful. Don't try to deal with this problem alone. Unfortunately, the obesity epidemic is not going away soon (we wish that it would), but you will be hearing more about the laws as well as receiving more duties to add to your lists. That is why we came together to provide you with the needed tools. We appeal to your knowledge to maintain or get to a healthy weight, delegate and build strong teams, and WATCH YOUR STRESS.

Strategies for Coping With Stress

Queen and Queen (2004), in their best-selling book *The Frazzled Teacher's Wellness Plan*, found that stress is a major part of the school culture. These topics and activities are beyond the scope of this book, but we have provided the outline model to help you. By going to www.frazzledteachers.com, you will be able to get relevant information to assist you in developing an individualized plan for coping with stress (see Figure 5.1). With your stress under

Figure 5.1   Developing a Personal Stress Management Plan

A. LEVEL I. Prevention Techniques I Will Use

    1.

    2.

    3.

    4.

    5.

B. LEVEL II. Leisure/Recreation Activities I Will Use

    1.

    2.

    3.

    4.

    5.

C. LEVEL III. Immediate Stress Relievers I Will Use

    1.

    2.

    3.

    4.

    5.

D. Situations, people, schedules, etc. that will assist me to be successful with Level I.

    1.

    2.

    3.

    4.

    5.

E. Situations, people, schedules, etc. that will try to prevent me from being successful with Level I.

    1.

    2.

    3.

    4.

    5.

(Continued)

Figure 5.1 (Continued)

F. Plan of action to correct problems listed in Item E.

1.

2.

3.

4.

5.

G. Situations, people, schedules, etc. that will assist me to be successful with Level II.

1.

2.

3.

4.

5.

H. Situations, people, schedules, etc. that will try to prevent me from being successful with Level II.

1.

2.

3.

4.

5.

I. Plan of action to correct problems listed in Item H.

1.

2.

3.

4.

5.

J. Situations, people, schedules, etc. that will assist me to be successful with Level III.

1.

2.

3.

4.

5.

K. Situations, people, schedules, etc. that will try to prevent me from being successful with Level III.

1.

2.

3.

4.

5.

L. Plan of action to correct problems listed in Item K.

1.

2.

3.

4.

5.

SOURCE: Copyright © 2005 by The Writer's Edge, Inc. Reprinted with permission from *The Frazzled Principal's Wellness Plan: Reclaiming Time, Managing Stress, and Creating a Healthy Lifestyle* by J. Allen Queen and Patsy S. Queen. Thousand Oaks, CA: Corwin Press, www.corwinpress.com.

control professionally and personally, you will be in shape to lead your school in helping us stamp out obesity in general and lead the way in stopping childhood obesity. Remember stress can impact not only your general health, but we are learning more from a medical standpoint about how the body deals with stress as related to metabolism, hunger, and other processes involved in eating. So to say the least, we will all be healthier if we learn to better manage our stress levels.

Stress reduction strategies recommended by Queen and Queen include the following:

- Direct strategies: identify the source of stress and take action to relieve it
- Palliative strategies: make stressful situations seem less stressful by looking at them in a different or reframed way
- Cognitive strategies: practice positive thinking
- Physical strategies: focus on good nutrition, exercises, sports, music, games, martial arts and desktop yoga. Developed

by Dr. Queen (Queen & Queen, 2004; Queen & Queen, 2005), desktop yoga can be done at home or at school. It consists of breathing techniques, poses, and movements to relax the body. Desktop yoga can be done alone, with teachers as part of a wellness program or class, or with students in a classroom. The program can easily fit into any instructional setting and is excellent for supporting physical fitness in instructional activities in many content areas.

What the Schools Need

Good health and wellness have enormous implications for prospective, beginning, and veteran school principals. Prospective administrators need to learn these content and wellness skills *before* they assume a leadership position. Practicing administrators need opportunities to participate in seminars on nutrition, wellness, and time and stress management. Progressive school systems will provide incentives for principals to become physically fit and learn to manage their stress levels. Just as with some businesses, gym memberships and professionals for special after school sessions, such as yoga, aerobics, weight lifting, or resistance training, will be provided.

School districts should make these opportunities available to faculty and staff members as well. Improved health will improve attendance and performance. These indirect actions will be picked up by students.

We strongly believe there are direct relationships between the levels of overall health and wellness of the adults in the school that have numerous effects on students. The daily wear and tear of negative stress take their toll mentally, emotionally, and physically. School leaders must remember to put their nutritional needs and physical fitness as a top priority and to keep a check on stress levels. You have learned in this book that these concepts are part of the same problem. As we stated earlier, principals must be the leaders and role models. Take our advice and see your life and the lives of everyone you touch improve. Master the information and skills. Today is a new day. We wish you success!

Resource A

*Nutritional and Physical
Fitness Survey for Grades 3–5*

We need your help. Please answer the following questions so we can learn more about you. **Please DO NOT WRITE YOUR NAME on this page**. We hope you and other boys and girls will help us learn more about the foods you like to eat. Please mark an X in the box that is your best answer.

Be sure to mark only one box for questions 1, 2, 3, and 4.

1. I am a   ❏ boy   ❏ girl

2. I am currently in the   ❏ 3rd   ❏ 4th   ❏ 5th
                                 grade   grade   grade

3. On my report card I get   ❏ *All A's*   ❏ *A's and B's*
                               ❏ *B's and C's*   ❏ *C's and D's*

4. When I think about school   ❏ I feel happy.   ❏ I feel sad.

(Continued)

(Continued)

Please place an X in the box to answer each question below.

1. I think I am   ❑ skinny   ❑ fat

2. I think I am   ❑ healthy   ❑ not healthy

3. I want to be   ❑ skinny   ❑ fat

4. I want to be   ❑ healthy   ❑ not healthy

5. In the morning   ❑ I never eat   ❑ I always eat
                                            breakfast   breakfast
                                         ❑ I sometimes
                                            eat breakfast

6. If you eat breakfast, put the   _____ Cold cereal (ex., Wheaties,
   number 1 next to the food you   corn flakes)
   like for breakfast the best. Place   _____ Hot cereal (ex., oatmeal)
   the number 2 next to the   _____ Eggs or eggs with meat
   breakfast food you like the next   (ex., bacon/sausage/ham)
   best. Now put the number 3   _____ Fast food sandwich
   beside the food you like   (ex., Hardee's, McDonald's)
   for breakfast next best. If you   _____ Fresh fruit (ex.,
   don't like breakfast, put an X in   banana, apple)
   the last place that says, "I don't   _____ Breakfast pastry (ex., Pop
   like breakfast."   Tart, honey bun)
                                         _____ Yogurt or milk
                                         _____ I don't like breakfast

7. If you skip breakfast sometimes,   ❑ Not hungry in the early
   what is the reason? Mark an   morning
   X in only *one* box for   ❑ Food not ready to eat
   your answer.   ❑ Nobody at home eats
                                            breakfast
                                         ❑ Could not go by McDonald's
                                            or Burger King

8. If you have or could have   _____ Yogurt or milk
   recess or a break before lunch   _____ Fresh fruit or juice
   at school, put the number 1 next   _____ Crackers or cookies
   to what you would get. What   _____ Chips
   would be your next choice? Put   _____ Soft drink
   the number 2 by that food or   _____ Water
   more choice after drink. If you
   could have one 1 and 2, what
   would be number 3? Put
   number 3 by that food or drink.

9. Where do you get lunch at school?

❑ I don't eat lunch.
❑ I bring lunch from home that my parents fixed.
❑ I buy lunch and eat in the cafeteria.
❑ I bring "Lunchables" to school for lunch.
❑ I bring lunch from home that I fixed.

10. Do you feel you have enough time to eat lunch at school?

❑ Yes   ❑ No

If NO, how much more time do you need?

❑ 15 minutes   ❑ 20 minutes or more

11. Put the number 1 next to the food that you would most likely eat for lunch at school. What would be your next choice? Put the number 2 beside that food. Let's choose another food. What would be number 3 for you? Place a 3 by the food and go ahead and put number 4 by the next best food you would choose. You will leave several foods without any numbers . . . that is OK.

_____ Meat with vegetables in the cafeteria
_____ A meat sandwich from home or the cafeteria
_____ Another kind of sandwich from home or the cafeteria
_____ Pizza in the cafeteria
_____ Burger and fries in the cafeteria
_____ Food from the cafeteria salad bar
_____ Fresh fruit from home or cafeteria
_____ Taco or potato bar in the cafeteria

12. Do you ever eat a snack after school?

❑ No
❑ Sometimes
❑ Each day

13. Put a number (1–7) by each of the food items. Start with number 1 for the food that you would most likely have for an afterschool snack and end with number 7 for the one that you would least likely have after school.

❑ A fast food item (burger, fries, taco)
❑ A soft drink
❑ A candy bar or other type of candy
❑ Peanut butter in a sandwich
❑ Food machine item (chips, cookies)
❑ Fresh fruit or vegetable (ex., apple, celery sticks)
❑ Milk or yogurt

(Continued)

(Continued)

14. On most school nights, where do you eat dinner or the evening meal?
- ❏ At home with other family members
- ❏ At home, but not as a group with family members
- ❏ "On the go" in the car
- ❏ Don't usually eat an evening meal, just snack while doing homework or watching TV

15. How often do you eat vegetables and fruit as part of your evening meal?
- ❏ Every day
- ❏ 1 day each week
- ❏ 2–3 times each week
- ❏ Almost never

16. How often do you eat baked or grilled meat (not fried) as part of your evening meal?
- ❏ Every day
- ❏ 1 day each week
- ❏ 2–3 times each week
- ❏ Almost never

17. Who cooks your evening meal *most of the time*?
- ❏ Mom or Dad
- ❏ I do it myself
- ❏ Sister, brother, or grandmother
- ❏ A restaurant or fast food place

18. In which school or community sports do you participate? (place an X by all that apply)
- ❏ Tennis
- ❏ Soccer
- ❏ Football
- ❏ Volleyball
- ❏ Swimming
- ❏ Basketball
- ❏ I do not participate in a sport
- ❏ Wrestling
- ❏ Golf
- ❏ Baseball
- ❏ Track and Field
- ❏ Other (please list)
  _____

19. How many times during a week do you exercise for at least 30 minutes to 1 hour?
- ❏ Every day
- ❏ 2–3 times a week
- ❏ 1–2 times a week
- ❏ 1 time a week
- ❏ Almost never

20. Put a number (1–10) by each activity. Start with number 1 for the one that you like the most and end with number 10 for the one that you like the least.

    _____ Running or jogging
    _____ Dancing
    _____ Yoga or stretching
    _____ Martial arts (karate, judo, kung fu, etc.)
    _____ Swimming
    _____ Pool exercises, like water aerobics
    _____ Lifting weights
    _____ Using weights and machines in the gym
    _____ Exercise classes
    _____ Walking
    _____ Other (please list _____)

21. How would you respond to this statement: "I am in excellent physical health."

❑ Agree strongly
❑ Agree somewhat
❑ Neither agree nor disagree
❑ Disagree somewhat
❑ Strongly disagree

Is there anything you would like to tell us about your eating or the sports you do?

Please write it in the blank space below. Thank you.

Resource B

Nutritional and Physical Fitness Survey for Grades 6–12

Dear Student,

We are asking you to spend a few minutes to complete a survey about some of your eating habits. Please DO NOT SIGN YOUR NAME or give any information other than what is asked in each of the items. Completing this survey is VOLUNTARY and you are NOT REQUIRED to participate. We value your opinion, and your assistance will help us improve our message to students and to better develop programs for students in the future.

Please describe yourself.

1. I am a   ❑ male   ❑ female

2. I am currently in grade   ❑ 6 ❑ 7 ❑ 8 ❑ 9 ❑ 10 ❑ 11 ❑ 12
   ❑ other grade, which is _____

3. I consider myself to be
   - ❑ Asian or Pacific Islander
   - ❑ Native American
   - ❑ White, Non-Hispanic
   - ❑ Black, Non-Hispanic
   - ❑ Hispanic

4. I consider myself to be
   - ❑ an average student
   - ❑ a successful Honors, AP, or IB student
   - ❑ an above average student

(Continued)

(Continued)

5. After high school
   graduation, I plan to
   - ❑ attend a community college
   - ❑ attend a college or university
   - ❑ start a full-time job
   - ❑ join the military
   - ❑ I do not plan to finish high school

Please pick the best choice to complete each of the following items about your eating and exercise habits.

1. I consider myself to be
   - ❑ underweight
   - ❑ slightly overweight
   - ❑ normal weight
   - ❑ very overweight

2. I try to lose weight
   - ❑ all the time
   - ❑ once a year
   - ❑ once a month
   - ❑ never

3. In the morning
   - ❑ I eat breakfast every day
   - ❑ I rarely eat breakfast
   - ❑ I eat breakfast about once a week
   - ❑ I eat breakfast 2–3 times a week

4. Put a number (1–9) by each of the breakfast foods. Start with number 1 for the one that you like the most and end with number 9 for the one that you like the least.
   - __ Cold cereal (ex., Wheaties, corn flakes)
   - __ Hot cereal (ex., oatmeal)
   - __ Eggs or eggs with meat (ex., bacon/sausage/ham)
   - __ Fast food sandwich (ex., Hardee's, McDonald's)
   - __ Fresh fruit (ex., banana, apple)
   - __ Breakfast bar (ex., Granola, Special K)
   - __ Breakfast pastry (ex. Pop Tart, honey bun)
   - __ Bagel or toast
   - __ Yogurt or milk

5. If you skip breakfast (even once), what is the *most common* reason?
   - ❑ Not hungry in the early morning
   - ❑ Food not readily available
   - ❑ Don't like traditional breakfast foods

6. Put a number (1–5) by each of the foods. Start with number 1 for the one that you would most like to have as a midmorning snack and end with number 5 for the one that you would least like to have as a midmorning snack.

_____ Yogurt or milk
_____ Fresh fruit or juice
_____ Crackers or cookies
_____ Chips
_____ Soft drink

7. Where do you eat lunch most of the time during the school day?

❑ Don't eat lunch
❑ Bring lunch from home and eat lunch in the cafeteria
❑ Buy lunch and eat in the cafeteria
❑ Buy vending food or bring lunch and eat in commons area

8. How much time are you allowed for lunch at school? _____ minutes
Is this enough time? ❑ Yes ❑ No

If not, how much time do you need? _____

9. Put a number (1–8) by each of the foods. Start with number 1 for the food that you would most likely eat for lunch at school and end with number 8 for the one that you would least likely eat for your school lunch.

_____ Meat with vegetable/fruit cafeteria offering
_____ A meat sandwich from home or the cafeteria
_____ Another kind of sandwich from home or the cafeteria
_____ Pizza cafeteria offering
_____ Burger and fries cafeteria offering
_____ Items from the cafeteria salad bar
_____ Fresh fruit from home or cafeteria offering
_____ Taco or potato bar from the cafeteria

10. About how often do you eat an afterschool snack?

❑ Daily
❑ Once a week
❑ Two to three times a week
❑ Almost never

(Continued)

(Continued)

---

11. Put a number (1–8) by each of the food items. Start with number 1 for the food that you would most likely have for an afterschool snack and end with number 8 for the one that you would least likely have after school.

❑ A fast food item (burger, fries, taco)
❑ A soft drink
❑ A candy bar or other type of candy
❑ Peanut butter in a sandwich or crackers
❑ Vending machine item (chips, cookies)
❑ Fresh fruit or vegetable (ex., apple, celery sticks.)
❑ Milk or yogurt
❑ A meat sandwich

12. On most school nights, where do you usually eat dinner or the evening meal?

❑ At home with other family members
❑ At home, but not as a group with family members
❑ At work
❑ "On the go" in the car
❑ Don't usually eat an evening meal, just snack while doing homework or watching TV

13. How often do you eat vegetables and fruit as part of your evening meal?

❑ Daily
❑ Once a week
❑ 2–3 times a week
❑ Almost never

14. How often do you eat baked or grilled meat (not fried) as part of your evening meal?

❑ Daily
❑ Once a week
❑ 2–3 times a week
❑ Almost never

15. Who prepares your evening meal *most of the time*?

❑ Parent
❑ I do it myself
❑ Other family member
❑ A restaurant or fast food chain

---

16. In which school- or community-sponsored sports do you participate? (check all that apply)

❏ Tennis
❏ Soccer
❏ Football
❏ Volleyball
❏ Swimming
❏ Baseball
❏ I do not participate in a sport

❏ Wrestling
❏ Golf
❏ Basketball
❏ Track and Field
❏ Other (please list)

_____

17. How many times during a week do you exercise for at least 30 minutes to 1 hour?

❏ Every day
❏ 2–3 times a week
❏ 1–2 times a week
❏ 1 time a week
❏ Almost never

18. Put a number (1–10) by each activity. Start with number 1 for the one that you like the most and end with number 10 for the one that you like the least.

_____ Running or jogging
_____ Dancing
_____ Yoga
_____ Martial arts (karate, judo, kung fu, etc.)
_____ Swimming
_____ Pool exercises, like water aerobics or deep-water jogging
_____ Lifting free weights
_____ Muscle training using weights and machines in the gym
_____ Aerobic exercise classes or tapes
_____ Walking
_____ Other (please list _____)

19. How would you respond to this statement: "I am in excellent physical condition."

❏ Agree strongly
❏ Agree somewhat
❏ Neither agree nor disagree
❏ Disagree somewhat
❏ Strongly disagree

Please write a short response to the questions below:

Medical researchers have concluded that a larger percentage of American children, adolescents, and young adults have become overweight or obese in the past 10–15 years; do you believe this to be true? Why or why not? And if you agree, what do you think has caused this problem to occur? What can you do to help stop it?

Do you have any other ideas about improving the epidemic of childhood obesity?

Thank you for completing our survey.

Resource C

Approximate Calories Burned Per Hour

Approximate Calories Burned Per Hour					
Average Weight	*100 lb*	*125 lb*	*150 lb*	*175 lb*	*200 lb*
1. Bicycling: >20 mph	792	990	1188	1386	1584
2. Bicycling: 12–13.9 mph	384	480	576	672	768
3. Bowling:	144	180	216	252	288
4. Golf: carrying clubs	264	330	396	462	528
5. Handball: general	576	720	864	1008	1152
6. Hiking: cross-country	288	360	432	504	576
7. Jumping Rope	480	600	720	840	960
8. Racquetball: casual	336	420	504	588	672
9. Tennis: general	336	420	504	588	672
10. Walk/Jog: jog <10 min	288	360	432	504	576
11. Walk: 17 min/mi	192	240	288	336	384
12. Swimming	288	360	432	504	576
13. Swimming: laps, vigorous	480	600	720	840	960
14. Aerobics, Step: high impact	480	600	720	840	960
15. Aerobics, Step: low impact	336	420	504	588	672
16. Aerobics: high impact	336	420	504	588	672
17. Aerobics: low impact	264	330	396	462	528
18. Aerobics: water	192	240	288	336	384

(Continued)

(Continued)

Approximate Calories Burned Per Hour					
Average Weight	100 lb	125 lb	150 lb	175 lb	200 lb
19. Bicycling, Stationary: moderate	336	420	504	588	672
20. Bicycling, Stationary: vigorous	504	630	756	882	1008
21. Stair Step Machine: general	288	360	432	504	576
22. Stretching, Hatha Yoga	192	240	288	336	384
23. Weight Lifting: general	144	180	216	252	288
24. Weight Lifting: vigorous	288	360	432	504	576
25. Boxing: sparring	432	450	648	756	864
26. Martial Arts: karate, kickboxing	480	600	720	840	960
27. Tai Chi	192	240	288	336	384
28. Dancing: disco, ballroom	264	330	396	462	528
29. Dancing: fast, ballet, twist	288	360	432	504	576
30. Gardening: general	216	270	324	378	432

SOURCE: U.S. Department of Veterans Affairs.

Resource D

USDA Label Definitions

Fat Free

Must contain less than ½ gram of fat per serving

Low Fat

Must contain less than 1 gram of saturated fat per serving and not more than 15% of calories can derive from saturated fat

Reduced Fat

Must contain 25% less fat than the regular product

Light

Must contain 50% less fat than the regular product

Reduced Sugar

Means at least 25% less sugar per serving than the regular food

High Fiber

Means 5 grams or more per serving, plus the food must either meet low-fat standards or indicate the total fat content next to the high-fiber claim

Good Source of Fiber

Means 2.5 to 4.9 grams per serving

No Cholesterol

Means the product contains 2 milligrams or less of cholesterol per serving, but it may contain up to 2 grams of saturated fat, which can raise blood cholesterol

(Continued)

(Continued)

Low Calorie

Means 40 calories or less per 50 grams of the food

Low Cholesterol

Must contain no more than 20 milligrams of cholesterol and no more than 2 grams of saturated fat per serving

Calorie Free

Means less than 5 calories per serving

Reduced Cholesterol

Must contain 75% less cholesterol than the regular product

Sodium Free

Means less than 140 milligrams of sodium per 50 grams of food

2% or Low-Fat Milk

Contains 38% of calories from fat and 4.7 grams of fat per 8-ounce glass

Low Sodium

Means less than 140 milligrams of sodium per 50 grams of the food

1% Milk

Contains 22% less calories from fat and 2.5 grams of fat per 8-ounce glass

Sugarless

Means contains no sucrose, but can contain other sugars such as corn syrup, dextrose, levulose, sorbitol, mannitol, maltitol, xylitol, or natural sweeteners at less than ½ gram per serving

Skim Milk

Contains 4% of calories from fat and 0.4 grams of fat per 8-ounce glass

SOURCE: Adapted from the U.S. Department of Agriculture.

References

Action for Healthy Kids. (2004). *The learning connection: The value of improving nutrition and physical activity in our schools.* Retrieved August 22, 2006, from http://www.actionforhealthykids.org

Akos, P., Queen, A., & Lineberry, C. (2005). *Promoting a successful transition to middle school.* Larchmont, NY: Eye on Education.

American Psychiatric Association. (2000). Practice guidelines for the treatment of patients with eating disorders (revision). *American Journal of Psychiatry, 157*(1 Suppl.), 1–39.

Americans experiencing pandemic of obesity, says director of Centers for Disease and Control in Atlanta (2003, February 21). The University of Georgia Public Affairs News Bureau. Retrieved April 26, 2006, from http://www.uga.edu/news/newsbureau/releases/2003releases/0303/030221gerberding.html

Andersen, K., Caldwell, D., Dunn, C., Hoggard, L., Thaxton, S., & Thomas, C. (2004). *Eat smart: NC's recommended standards for all foods available in school.* Raleigh: North Carolina DHHS, NC Division of Public Health.

Brownell, K., & Horgen, K. (2004). *Food fight: The inside story of the food industry: America's obesity crisis and what we can do about it.* New York: McGraw-Hill.

California Department of Education. (2002). Department pamphlet.

Caspersen, C. J., Powell, K. E., & Christenson, G. M. (1985). Physical activity, exercise, and physical fitness: definitions and distinctions for health-related research. *Public Health Reports, 100,* 126–131.

Center for Health and Health Care in Schools. (2003). *What's happening in your school? Survey results 2003.* Washington, DC: School of Public Health and Health Services, George Washington University Medical Center.

Centers for Disease Control. (1996). *Guidelines for school health programs to promote lifelong healthy eating* (MMWR series). Atlanta, GA: Author.

Center for Science in the Public Interest. (2006). *School foods report.* Retrieved August 18, 2006, from http://www.cspinet.org/new/ school_foods_report_card.pdf

Datar, A. & Strum, R. (2004, September). Physical education in elementary school and body mass index: Evidence from the Early Childhood Longitudinal Study. *American Journal of Public Health, 94,* 1501–1506.

Department of Health and Human Services. (2001). *The surgeon general's call to action to prevent and decrease overweight and obesity.* Rockville, MD: Author.

Department of Health and Human Services. (2004, August 16). *School-based interventions to prevent obesity* [PA Number PA-04-145]. Washington, DC: Author.

Department of Health and Human Services. (2005). *The dietary guidelines for Americans 2005.* Washington, DC: Author.

Dietz, W. H., Bland, M. G., Gortmaker, S. L., Molloy, M., & Schmid, T. L. (2002, Fall). Policy tools for the childhood obesity epidemic. *Journal of Law and Medical Ethics, 30*(Suppl. 3), 83–87.

Economic Research Service, U.S. Department of Agriculture (2003, April 22). *Economics of obesity workshop.* Papers presented at the meeting of the Economic Research Service, USDA, Washington, DC.

Greer, C. H. (1973). *The great school legend: A revisionist interpretation of American public education.* New York: Basic Books.

Harvey-Berino, J., & Rourke, J. (2003). Obesity prevention in pre-school Native American children. *Obesity Research 11*(5), 606–611.

James, J., Thomas, P., Cavan, D., & Kerr, D. (2004). Preventing childhood obesity by reducing consumption of carbonated drinks: Cluster randomized controlled trial. *British Medical Journal, 328,* 1237.

National Center for Chronic Disease Prevention and Health Promotion. (n.d.). *Healthy Youth! Health Topics: Nutrition: School health guidelines.* Retrieved August 22, 2006, from http://www.cdc.gov/healthyyouth/ nutrition/guidelines/summary.htm

National Center for Health Statistics. (n.d.). *Prevalence of Overweight Among Children and Adolescents: United States, 1999–2002.* Hyattsville, MD: U.S. Department of Health and Human Services. Retrieved August 22, 2006, from http://www.cdc.gov/nchs/products/ pubs/pubd/hestats/overwght99.htm

Ogden, C. L., Flegal, K. M., Carroll, M. D., & Johnson, C. L. (2002, October 9). Prevalence and trends in overweight among U.S. children and adolescents, 1999–2000. *Journal of the American Medical Association, 288*(14), 1728–1732.

Queen, J. A., & Queen P. S. (2004). *The frazzled teacher's wellness plan: A five step program for reclaiming time, managing stress, and creating a healthy lifestyle.* Thousand Oaks, CA: Corwin.

Queen, J. A., & Queen, P. S. (2005). *The frazzled principal's wellness plan: Reclaiming time, managing stress, and creating a healthy lifestyle.* Thousand Oaks, CA: Corwin.

Robert Wood Johnson Foundation. (2003, December). *Healthy schools for healthy living.* Princeton, NJ: Author.

Satcher, D. (2004). *Action for Healthy Kids, the learning connection: The value of improving nutrition and physical activity in our schools.* Available from www.actionforhealthykids.org

Shipman, N., Martin, J., McKay, A., & Anastasi, R. (1987). *Effective time-management techniques for school administrators.* Englewood Cliffs, NJ: Prentice-Hall.

Tanner, D., & Tanner, L. (2007). *Curriculum development: Theory into practice* (4th ed.). Upper Saddle River, NJ: Merrill/Prentice Hall.

Tirozzi, G., & Ferrandino, V. (2001, January 31). How do you reinvent a principal? [Electronic version]. *Education Week.* Retrieved April 26, 2006, from http://www.naesp.or/ContentLoad.do?contentId=902

Tufts University School of Nutrition. (1995). *Center on Hunger, Poverty, and Nutrition Policy: The link between nutrition and cognitive development in children.* Medford, MA: Author.

U.S. Department of Agriculture. (2001). *Foods sold in competition with USDA school meal programs: A report to Congress.* Washington, DC: Author.

U.S. Department of Veteran Affairs, National Center for Health Promotion and Disease Prevention. (n.d.). *Move! Calories Burned During Activities.* Retrieved August 22, 2006, from http://www.move.va.gov/download/handout/PhysicalActivity/P03_CaloriesBurnedDuringActivities.pdf

World Health Organization (WHO). (2003). *Obesity and overweight.* Retrieved April 26, 2006, from http://www.who.int/hpr.nph/docs/gs-obesity.pdf

Index

Absenteeism:
  nutrition and, 20
  School Breakfast Program
    and, 21, 101–102
  stress and, 65
  unhealthy weight and, 1, 101
Academic achievements, 25
  body shapes and, 8
  principals and, 24, 25, 26, 27,
    52–53
  school grades and, 108–109
  unhealthy weight and, 1,
    18–21, 101
Accountability, 27–28
Action plans, xii, 57, 72, 108
Administrators:
  role models and, 24, 29, 56,
    58, 63, 77, 99
  stress and, 64, 114
  training and, 45
  See also Principals; Teachers
Advertisements, food, 16
African Americans, 10, 13, 18
Afterschool activities, 49, 64
Akos, P., 66
Alabama, 109
American Academy of
  Pediatrics, 18
American Cancer Society, 48, 94
American Dietetic Association,
  48, 94

American Heart Association,
  48, 94
American Pediatric Society, 7
American School Food Services
  Association, 48, 94
Americans Experiencing
  Pandemic, x
Andersen, K., 11
Arizona, 109
Arkansas, 51, 109
Art skills, 82–83, 84–85, 90, 91
Asians, 8
Association of Supervision
  and Curriculum
  Development, 20
At-risk students, 25, 98–99
Attendance, 20, 21, 101–102

Barriers, 55–56, 108
  health care providers
    and, 69
  modeling behaviors and, 63
  prejudice and, 59–60
  principals and, 56
  school boards/parent organi-
    zations and, 68–69
  schools and, 61–63
  stress/overeating and, 63–66
  students and, 59
  transitions/resistance and,
    66–68

Behaviors, xi
  body shapes and, 8
  change and, 29, 44–45,
    58, 97
  defensive, 99
  discipline and, 100
  emotions and, 42
  fun and, 48, 96
  parents and, 57
  role models and, 56
  stress and, 65. *See also* Stress
Bland, M. G., 103
Blood pressure, 12, 38,
    39, 65, 73
Body fat, 5, 11, 12, 38, 40
Body images, 6
Body Mass Index (BMI), ix
  educators and, 13–14
  pediatric charts and, 7–8
  principal's team and, 73
  unhealthy weight and, 97–98
Body shapes, 8
Bone health, 16
Breakfast, 30, 33, 46, 62,
    101, 102
Brownell, K., ix, 10, 103
Bullying, 98–99, 100
Burnout, 64, 110

Cafeterias, 11
  CDC guidelines and, 48
  change and, 95
  community responsibilities
    and, 103–104
  competitive foods and, 61
  fast foods and, 15
  food choices and, 15, 37
  food service directors and,
    96–97
  nutrition education and, 46
  nutrition messages in, 50, 78
  self-supporting, 62
Caldwell, D., 11

California, 19, 51, 109
Calories:
  burning of, 127–128
  choices and, 36
  counting, 41–42
  exercise and, 38
  fat/muscle and, 39
  meals and, 41
  portions and, 35–36, 41
  scheduled eating
    and, 34
Cancer, 35, 103
  See also Diseases
Carbonated drinks, 103
  See also Soft drinks
Carroll, M. D., 7
Caspersen,, 48
Cavan, D., 103
Center for Health and Health
    Care in Schools, 13
Center for Science in the Public
    Interest, 109
Centers for Disease Control
    (CDC), ix, 3, 45
  exercise and, 18
  health programs and,
    76, 94, 95
  pediatric charts and, 7
  school-based programs and,
    45–47
Change:
  anxiety and, 66
  behaviors and, 29, 97
  criticism and, 59
  leadership and, 104
  lifestyles and, 32
  obesity and, 6
  parents and, 56–58, 58
  planning for, 66–67
  principals and, 29, 56
  resistance and, 95
  school culture and, 75
  school events and, 62

teachers and, 99
transitions and, 66–68
weight and, 96
Child Nutrition Act, x, 78, 109
Cholesterol, 12, 38, 39
Cigarette smoking, 104–105
Civic organizations, 24, 50, 53
Class participation, 21, 101–102
Classrooms:
    healthy weight habits and, xi
    integrating health and well-
        ness into, xii, 79–82
    nutrition messages in,
        50, 78
Coding procedures, 82
Committee on Health, 3
Committees, nutrition
    advisory, 47–48
Communications, 82–83,
    85, 86–87
Computer skills, 82–83, 84, 85,
    87, 89, 90, 91, 92, 93
Connecticut, 51
Consumer Information
    Center, 94
Cooking skills, 82–83
Counselors, 59–60, 97
Critical thinking, 85
Culture:
    longevity and, 9
    obesity and, 6
    role models and, 56
    stress and, 110
Curriculum:
    change and, 44
    health and, 95–96
    principals and, 27
    school activity goals and, 49
    school environments
        and, 45
    short-changing of, 63
    structural barriers and,
        61–63

Data:
    lack of, 50, 95
    most recent
        epidemiological, 104
    outcomes and, 45
    principals and, 97
    student teams and, 77
    U.S. Department of Education
        and, 102–103
Datar, A., 102
Decision making, 65, 73
    See also Leadership
Department of Health and
    Human Services,
    44, 45, 103
Department of Public
    Instruction, x
Depression:
    exercise and, 40
    stress and, 64
    unhealthy weight and, 99
Desktop yoga, 113–114
Desserts, 8
    See also Snacks
Diabetes, 6, 12, 103
Diet plans, 37
Dietary guidelines, 101 (figure)
Dietitians, 62, 74, 96,
    97, 105
Dietz, W. H., 3, 12, 103
Discipline problems, 1, 6
Discrimination, 8, 18,
    59–60, 102
Diseases, 11
    cancer, 35, 103
    exercise and, 38, 39, 40
    fruits/vegetables and, 15, 35
    HIV/AIDS, 103
    unhealthy eating and, 102
    unhealthy weight and,
        11, 19, 103
Doctors *See* Physicians
Dunn, C., 11

Early interventions, 12
Eastin, D., 19
Eating disorders, 35, 42
Eating habits:
    behavior modification and, 45
    change and, 30–31
    learning of, 16
    principles and, 30–31
    stress and, 110–111, 113
    time and, 42
    women in the workplace and,
        9–10
Eating out, 9, 15, 37, 48, 51
    See also Fast foods
Eating times, 8
Economic Research Service,
        U.S. Department of
        Agriculture, 9
Education, xi, 10, 18
Educators:
    eating habits and, 14, 30–31
    identification process and, 13
    See also Administrators;
        Teachers
Emotional development, xii
    eating and, 42
    principals and, 27
    stress and, 63–64, 65
English, 79–80
Environments, 108
    CDC reports and, 47
    change and, 45
    healthy weight habits and, xi
    negative exercise zones and, 68
    principals and, 24, 52–53
    schools and, 104–105
    self-esteem and, 98–99
    unhealthy weight and, 4
Essential Truths, x, xi, xii
Exercise, xi
    action plans and, 72
    aerobic/anaerobic activity
        and, 41

aging and, 11
behavior modification and, 45
benefits of, 38–39, 40–41
crosstraining and, 39
definition of, 48–49
diaries and, 33
establishments and, 50
information and, 3
lack of, 20
medical costs and, 18
physical education instructors
    and, 96
planning and, 37–41
school activity goals and, 49
schools and, 8
stress and, 113
success and, 6, 32–33
weight loss and, 30
women in the workplace
    and, 10
See also Physical activity
Exercise equipment, 40
Exercise plans, 3

Families:
    budgets and, 14–15
    change and, 58
    eating habits and, 16
    fast food and, 35
    unhealthy weight and,
        4, 13–14, 56–58
    women in the workplace
        and, 9–10
    See also Parents
Fast foods, 9–10, 15, 36
    alternatives and, 32
    budgets and, 35
    change and, 30
    nutrition advisory
        committees and, 48
    portions and, 36
    unhealthy weight
        and, 9–10

Fat, body, 5, 11, 12, 38, 40
Ferrandino, V., 28, 99, 103
Flegal, K. M., 7
Food and beverage industry, 24
Food and Nutrition Information
   Center, 94
Food choices, 45
Food preparation, 10, 14, 15
Food prices, 9–10
Food pyramid, 16 (figure), 17
   (figure), 89, 91, 93
Food service directors, 96–97
Food service personnel, 45
Fruits:
   calories and, 35
   diseases and, 15
   food pyramid and, 16 (figure),
      17 (figure)
   nutrition and, 14
Funding, 24–25, 50, 51,
   53, 62, 75
Fundraisers, 109

Galbraith, J. K., 55
Genetics, 4–5, 11, 36, 58
Geography, 52, 82–83, 84,
   85, 86, 90, 92, 93
Gerberding, J., ix
Gortmaker, S. L., 103
Greer, C. H., 26

Habits:
   behavior modification
      and, 45
   change and, 11–12, 30, 57,
      66, 95
   improving, 50
   parental involvement and, 14
   portions and, 36
Health, 44
   balanced meals and, 16
   curriculum and, 95–96
   exercise and, 38, 39

foods and, 46
goals and, 31, 49
parents and, 57
principals and, 28, 29, 110
stress and, 64, 110. *See also*
   Stress
structural barriers and,
   61–63
teachers and, 72
training and, 44
unhealthy weight and, 1
Health and Human
   Services, 46
Health care, 45–46, 104
Health care providers, 14, 69
Health committees, 47–48
Health departments,
   48, 50, 74
Health insurance, 69
Healthy Active Children Policy,
   93–94
Healthy Children, Healthy
   Schools, 23
Healthy weight, 6, 8, 14
Heart disease, 6, 12, 38,
   39, 65, 103
High blood pressure, 38, 65
Hispanics, 10, 13, 18
History, 44, 52, 79–80,
   82–83, 93
Hoggard, L., 11
Homeostasis, 5
Horgen, K., ix, 10
Huckabee, M., 51

Integrated units, 79–82
International Food Information
   Council, 94

James, J., 103
Johnson, C. L., 7
Journals, 33, 40, 85,
   89, 90, 91, 93

Junk foods, 30–31
See also Fast foods

Kentucky, 109
Kerr, D., 103
Kindergartners, 102–103
Knowledge:
    laws and, 78
    nutritional/physical fitness
        and, 75
    testing and, 79
    unhealthy weight and,
        11, 16, 18
    weight loss and, 40

Language Arts, 82–83,
    84, 85–86, 93
Laws:
    being aware of, 77–78
    changes in, xii
    healthy foods and, 15
    leadership and, xi
Leadership, xi
    change and, 104
    principals and, x, 24,
        27, 110
    principal's team and, 73, 75
    stress and, 65, 114
    students and, 77
    wellness plans and, 108
Learning *See* Academic
    achievements
Lesson planning:
    information for parents
        and, 98
    nutrition and, 80–82
    physical activity and, 52–53
    principal's team and, 76
    student prejudice and, 59–60
Lifestyles, xi
    action plans and, 72
    behavior modification and,
        44–45

change and, 8, 31, 32
information and, 3
North Carolina and, 93–94
parental involvement
    and, 14
sedentary, 104
unhealthy weight and, 4
weight gain and, 5
Lineberry, C., 66
Longevity, 9, 29, 40
Low income, 14–15, 18
Lunch, 30, 33, 34, 46, 62

Magnabosco, J. L., 102
Mandates, 64, 108
Massachusetts, 52
Mathematics, 20, 44,
    79, 82, 86, 93
Max HR, 39
Meals, 16
Media, 50–52, 77, 97, 105
Medical problems, 12, 39
Medications, 12
Messaging, 50, 78
Modeling, 24, 29, 56,
    58, 63, 77, 99
Molloy, M., 103
Muscle mass:
    aging and, 11
    change and, 8
    childhood growth and, 6–7
    exercise and, 39
    lifestyles and, 5
Music, 79, 90–91, 113

National Association of
    Elementary School
    Principals, 28, 103
National Food Service
    Management Institute, 94
National Heart, Lung and Blood
    Institute Information
    Center, 94

National School Lunch Program, x, 62, 78

New Mexico, 109

Nighttime eating, 34–35, 42

No Child Left Behind Act, x, 27

North Carolina, 51–52, 93

Nurses:
  barriers and, 69
  BMI and, 98
  information and, 96
  messaging and, 78
  prejudice and, 59–60
  principal's team and, 73
  training and, 45

Nutrition, xi, 79–82
  academic achievements and, 19–20. *See also* Academic achievements
  action plans and, 72
  aging and, 11
  biomes for fifth grade and, 82–83, 84, 85, 91–92, 93
  CDC guideline for, 45–47
  change and, 11, 95. *See also* Change
  education and, 46
  food choices and, 14, 30, 34, 42
  food service directors and, 96–97
  ignorance and, 16, 18
  information and, 3
  parents and, 58
  plans and, 108
  school activity goals and, 49
  standards and, 109
  stress and, 113, 114
  wellness policies and, x, 78

Nutrition advisory committees, 47–48

Nutrition Education and Training Program, 76

Ogden, C. L., 7

Overeating, 63–66, 65, 110–111, 113

Overweight children, 5
  percentage of, 101 (figure)

Parent organizations, 68–69

Parent Teacher Association (PTA), 97

Parents:
  CDC guidelines and, 48
  change and, 15, 66, 95. *See also* Change
  eating habits and, 14
  exercise and, 18, 20
  food choices and, 9–10
  food preparation and, 15
  genetics and, 4
  ignorance and, 16, 18
  interventions and, 14
  Massachusetts and, 52
  menu options and, 97
  nutrition education and, 98
  outliving children, 6
  principals and, 24, 68
  resistance and, xi, 52, 56
  role models and, 107
  60% overweight, 56
  training and, 45
  unhealthy weight and, 2, 69
  wellness plans and, 108
  See also Familes

Pediatricians, 53

Pensions Subcommittee on Public Health, 3

Perdue, B. E., 51

Physical activity:
  behavior modification and, 44–45
  change and, 8, 11
  definition of, 49
  home and, 14

intergrating into classrooms
    and, 79
lesson planning and, 52–53
mandates and, 51
medical costs and, 18
North Carolina and, 93–94
parents and, 58, 98
principals and, 110
schools and, 8
sedentary occupations and, 9
unhealthy weight and, 5
weight gain and, 10
wellness policies and, x, 78
See also Exercise
Physical education:
    de-emphasis of, 68
    definition of, 49
    elimination of, 103
    fun and, 96
    kindergarten/first grade and,
        102–103
    school activity goals
        and, 49
    schools and, 8–9
    structural barriers and,
        61–63
Physical fitness:
    academic achievements
        and, 19
    faculties and, 108
    stress and, 114
    wellness plans and, 108
Physicians:
    barriers and, 69
    BMI and, 98
    eating habits and, 14
    exercise and, 39
    principal's team and, 73
    support from, 53
    unhealthy weight and, 18
Planning, 95
    See also Lesson planning;
        Wellness plans

Playtime, 8
    See also Recess
Politics, 68–69
Portion sizes, 15, 35–36,
    41, 42
Power Plan campaign, 51
Prejudice, 98–99
    academic achievements
        and, 18
    barriers and, 59–60
    discipline and, 100
    students and, xi, 59
    teachers and, 102
Prevention, xi, 103
    principals and, 23, 24, 26
    unhealthy weight and,
        6, 11, 19
Principals:
    action plans and, xii, 108.
        See also Action plans
    barriers and, 55–56. See also
        Barriers
    change and, 23, 56, 95.
        See also Change
    civic organizations and,
        24, 50, 53
    developing partnerships
        and, 50–52
    environments and, 52–53
    health and, 110
    leadership and, x, 104.
        See also Leadership
    messaging and, 78
    parents and, 68
    prejudice and, 59–60
    responsibility of, xi, 26,
        27, 28, 29
    role models and, xi, 24, 29,
        56, 58, 63, 77, 99, 107
    roles of, 28
    stress and, xii, 64, 65,
        110, 114
    student wellness and, 29

success and, 53
teachers and, 29, 43, 66
teams and, 72–75
training and, 44
weight loss and, 30–31
wellness plans and, 43
Professional organizations, 24

Queen, J. A., 20, 25,
    64, 110, 113
Queen, P. S., 25, 64,
    66, 110, 113

Rand Corporation, 102
Readiness scale, 66
Recess, 51
    elimination of, 103
    physical activity and, 8–9
    physical education instructors
        and, 96
    school activity goals and, 49
Responsibilities:
    communities and, 103–104
    parents and, 58
    principals and, xi, 26, 27,
        28, 29
    teachers and, xii, 80
Restaurants, 48, 51
Resting Metabolic Rate (RMR),
    41–42
Robert Wood Johnson
    Foundation, 19
Role models, xi, 24, 29, 56,
    58, 63, 77, 99, 107
Rubrics, 83, 93

Safety, 8, 39
Satcher, D., 20, 21, 103
Schmid, T. L., 103
School activity goals, 49
School boards, 68–69
School Breakfast Program,
    20, 21, 62

School-sanctioned events, 61, 78
Schools:
    depression and, 99.
        See also Depression
    environments and, 104–105
    exercise and, 8, 46
    grading of, 108–109
    negative exercise zones
        and, 68
    nutritional education and,
        46, 96
    physical education and, 108
    prevention and, 11.
        See also Prevention
    society and, 26, 28
    stress and, 110
Schumacher, D. S., 52
Science, 3, 44, 82–83,
    85, 86, 93
Self-barriers, 55, 59
    See also Barriers
Self-esteem, 98–99
    action plans and, 72
    physical fitness and, 19
    unhealthy weight and, 12, 18,
        19, 100, 102
Seven Cardinal Principles, 27
Smoking, 104–105
Snacks, 8, 14, 16, 30–31
Social skills, 4, 9, 18–21,
    26, 27, 83
Social studies, 44, 52, 79
Societal ills, 28
Soft drinks, 16, 35, 103
Special interest groups,
    24, 50–52
Standards:
    academic achievements
        and, 101
    leadership and, xi
    North Carolina and, 52
    nutrition and, 109
    principals and, 24, 25, 27

testing and, 20. *See also*
    Testing
themes and, 80
USDA and, 62
Stress, xi
    eating and, 35, 63–66,
        110–111, 113
    emotions and, 42, 65
    exercise and, 40
    managing, 110–114,
        111–113 (figure)
    physical fitness and, 19
    principals and, xii, 25, 110
    schools and, 110
    wellness plans and, 108
Strum, R., 102
Student achievements *See*
    Academic achievements
Success:
    action plans and, 72
    change and, 29–30, 32, 66
    early interventions
        and, 12
    exercise and, 39, 40
    goals and, 31
    healthy weight and, 6
    limited, 95
    parents and, 58
    principals and, 24, 25, 53, 55
Superintendents:
    change and, 95.
        See also Change
    60% overweight, 56
Surveys, 115–119,
    121–126
Sweets, 8

Tanner, D., 27
Tanner, L., 27
Tardiness, 21, 101–102
Task forces, 45
Teachers:
    activities and, 108

change and, 11–12, 66
food service directors and,
    96–97
health and, 11, 72
nutrition and, 18
prejudice and, 18, 59–60, 99,
    102. *See also* Prejudice
principals and, 24, 43, 66
responsibilities and,
    xii, 80
role models and,
    24, 29, 56, 58,
    63, 77, 99, 107
sensitive situation training
    and, 60
60% overweight, 56
societal ills and, 28
student wellness and, 29
training and, 45, 49–50
wellness plans and, 108
Team Nutrition, U.S. Department
    of Agriculture, 94, 95
Teams, 72–75
Teasing, 98–99
Television, 16, 18
    behavior modification and,
        44–45
    eating and, 36, 43
Tennessee, 109
Testing, 20
    academic achievements
        and, 101
    elimination of physical
        education and, 103
    knowledge and, 79
    learning environments
        and, 78
    nutrition and, 20
    principals and, 25, 27
    School Breakfast Program
        and, 21, 101–102
Texas, 51
Thaxton, S., 11

Third world countries, 5–6
Thomas, C., 11
Thomas, P., 103
Time management, 108
Training:
  pedestrian-safety and, 52
  principals and, 24, 43, 44
  sensitive situations and, 60
  staff and, 45
  teachers and, 49–50
Transitions, 66–68
Triglycerides, 12, 38
Tufts University School of
    Nutrition, 21

U.S. Department of
    Agriculture (USDA),
    9, 36, 76, 94, 96, 103
  breakfasts/lunches
    and, 62
  calories and, 36
  food pyramid and, 16 (Figure),
    17 (Figure)
  label definitions and,
    129–130
U.S. Department of Education,
    102–103

Vegetables:
  calories and, 35
  diseases and, 15
  food pyramid and, 16 (Figure),
    17 (Figure)
  nutrition and, 14
Vegetarians, 36
Vending machines, 11, 15, 77
  choices and, 30
  contracts and, 61–63
  grading of schools and, 109
  healthy choices and, 34
  North Carolina and, 51–52
  nutrition education and, 46
  principal's team and, 74

removing, 47
representatives and, 97
school-sponsored events
    and, 35
Volunteers, 59–60

Web sites, 76, 78, 80
  biomes for fifth grade
    and, 93
  BMI and, 98
  grading of schools and, 109
  managers and, 97
Weight gain:
  educators becoming aware
    of children's, 13–14
  food prices and, 9–10
  genetics and, 58
  lifestyles and, 5
  prevention of, 6, 11, 19
  women in the workplace
    and, 9–10
Weight loss:
  choices and, 30–31
  emotions and, 42
  exercise and, 3, 40
  food intake and, 9, 30
  muscle and, 38
  parents and, 56–58
  principals and, 29
  scheduled eating
    and, 34
  self-esteem and, 12
  structural barriers and,
    61–63
  structure and, 33
  success and, 32–33
Weight management:
  change and, 96. *See also*
    Change
  doctors and, 69
  parental involvement
    and, 14
  principals and, 110

Wellness plans, x, 43–44, 78,
    96–98, 108
  laws and, 78
  principals and, 43
  stress and, xii
Women:
  fruits/vegetables and, 15
  workplace and, 9–10

Women, Infants, and Children
    (WIC), 48, 75
World Health Organization
    (WHO), ix, 6
Writer's Edge, Inc., 113

Yoga, 19–20, 113–114